BIBLIOGRAPHY

OF THE

WRITINGS

OF

ALBERT PIKE

Albert Pike was the foremost Master of Masonic Wisdom.
Study this man. Read his writings.

Ray Baker Harris

ISBN 1-56459-448-3

PORTRAIT OF ALBERT PIKE

Painted by Charles Loring Elliott and first exhibited in New York City in 1844, when Albert Pike was 34 years of age. Bequeathed by Pike to the Supreme Council, it now hangs in the House of the Temple, Washington, D. C.

ALBERT PIKE STATUE

Memorial statue of Albert Pike, by sculptor Gilbert de Trentanove, stands in a triangle of government land which is part of the north plaza bordering the District of Columbia Municipal Building at 3rd and Indiana Avenue, only a block distant from the old House of the Temple where Albert Pike had lived during his last years. The heroic figure of Pike stands on a marble pedestal at the side of which is the bronze figure of a woman, representing Peace, in an attitude of mourning. Dedicated October 23, 1901.

FOREWORD

BY

ILL.·. LUTHER A. SMITH, 33°

SOVEREIGN GRAND COMMANDER

ALBERT PIKE became a Master Mason at almost exactly the halfway point in his long lifetime. He had already acquired an outstanding and unique reputation as a lawyer, jurist, editor, soldier, author and poet.

In April of 1857 the Supreme Council of the Ancient and Accepted Scottish Rite conferred on him its 33rd Degree Honorary, in recognition of nearly seven years of extraordinary Masonic zeal and accomplishment. From this moment and until the close of his life, Albert Pike devoted his great talents increasingly to Freemasonry and particularly to the Ancient and Accepted Scottish Rite. In his monumental work on the rituals he bequeathed to the Rite a substance and a purpose, and he made of the Degrees a scholarly procession of philosophical thought climactic in the concluding Degrees. From his talents as a lawyer and jurist, he gave sound form to the Statutes and law of the Rite; and his counsel and labors gave strength to its organizational structure. In Albert Pike's time the membership of the Scottish Rite was small indeed. It had quadrupled by the time of his death; and upon the firm foundation he established, its membership in the Southern Jurisdiction [33 States and U. S. territorial possessions] is today nearly half a million. There is no way to estimate the effect of his work upon the other Scottish Rite jurisdictions throughout the world, all of which are descended either directly or indirectly from our Supreme Council.

In addition to receiving the 33rd Degree, Albert Pike also in 1857 established the Scottish Rite Bodies at Little Rock, Arkansas. Consequently the centennial observance of that year is an important occasion in the Scottish Rite and for Freemasons generally.

As a partial observance of this centennial, we publish with pleasure a new edition of the *Bibliography of the Writings of Albert Pike,* edited by the Librarian of the Supreme Council, and based upon the previous edition prepared by his predecessor, the late William L. Boyden 33°, privately printed in 1921.

The bibliography in its entirety reflects the enormous and divers talent of Albert Pike in many fields apart from his fraternal interests, and should therefore be of wide interest and usefulness.

LUTHER A. SMITH
Sovereign Grand Commander

HOUSE OF THE TEMPLE,
WASHINGTON, D. C.

APRIL, 1957

INTRODUCTION

ANY NEW EDITION of the *Bibliography of the Writings of Albert Pike* must owe a primary acknowledgment to the first edition prepared by the late William L. Boyden in 1921. He became Librarian of the Supreme Council Library, founded by Albert Pike in 1888, only a few years after the founder's death. The present library was entirely recatalogued by him when it was moved to the newly constructed House of the Temple in 1915. All of the initial cataloguing, arranging and collating of Albert Pike materials, and the first arrangement of The Albert Pike Collection, was done by Mr. Boyden. His bibliography, therefore, was the product of nearly 30 years close association with these materials.

During the 35 years since then, however, new items have come to light and new information has required some changes in dates or other points of identification.

Although the sketch of Albert Pike's life presented here has been greatly enlarged from the brief one published in the first edition, it is still of necessity drawn in the most general terms. Many facts and many of Pike's activities and interests have had to be omitted.

The writings listed in this bibliography continue to be the principal source materials on the life of Albert Pike. Published biographical material remains limited. The chapter entitled "The Master Builder" in Charles S. Lobingier's [history of] *The Supreme Council,* 33°, 1931, is perhaps the most complete and accurate biographical presentation now in print, but is in no sense a definitive biography. *Albert Pike, A Biography,* by Fred W. Allsopp, 1928, brought together a wide assortment of biographical information but is essentially a record compiled by an admirer.

The most comprehensive biographical study of Albert Pike to be written thus far is a manuscript prepared by Professor Walter Lee Brown of the History Department of the University of Arkansas as a thesis in partial requirement for his Master's degree at the University of Texas. His work is enhanced by long and thorough research, a prose that reflects scholarship, with complete documentation and bibliography. It deals primarily, however, with Albert Pike's life apart from Freemasonry; and the Masonic treatment has been necessarily generalized. But if Professor Brown's work is published by a University press, as is contemplated, it will be the most comprehensive biography of Albert Pike thus far to appear in print.

Any student of Albert Pike's life in relation to his writings [apart from Masonry] will owe a debt to the more than five years of research done by Dr. Susan B. Riley, now Professor of English at the George Peabody College for Teachers, Nashville, Tennessee. Dr. Riley's thesis for the Degree of Doctor of Philosophy, 1934, was entitled *The Life and Works of Albert Pike to 1860*. No one else has more completely compiled Pike's uncollected verse. Her paper on *Albert Pike in Tennessee* [Tennessee Historical Quarterly, Vol. IX, No. 4, December 1950] documents a little known period in relation to his earlier and later life. We gratefully acknowledge Dr. Riley's assistance in preparing this new edition of the bibliography, particularly in the section for Poetry.

Another valuable and unpublished source of information on Albert Pike's Masonic writings is the collection of notes and indexes prepared from his extensive study over many years by Mr. Fred P. Farrar, 33°, of Miami, Florida. We are indebted to him especially for identification of the revisions and printings of Pike ritualistic material.

There is an abundance of printed material dealing with particular phases or fragments of Albert Pike's life, and periodical articles, by various authors. The most complete listing of them is to be found in Professor Brown's work. We have not attempted in this Bibliography to go beyond Albert Pike's own writings, published and unpublished.

R. B. H.

Heroic size bronze bust executed by sculptor U. S. J. Dunbar, placed on marble pedestal designed by architect John Russell Pope. It is located in front of the Albert Pike crypt in the House of the Temple.

ALBERT PIKE

1809 - 1891

ALBERT PIKE'S lifetime spanned the nineteenth century except for its first and its last decades. This was the great period of the beginnings and growth of the United States of America, a time of expanding frontiers, upheavals, trials and errors, and all the tragedies and the glories in the birth of a new nation. Through this dramatic panorama of our country's first century moved the majestic figure of Albert Pike—from the land of the Massachusetts Bay Colony, to the West and to the South—from the academic halls of New England, to the rigors of the frontier in western plains, deserts and mountains, to the economic, political and social transitions taking place in Arkansas and the South. A man of enormous talent, imposing physical appearance and strength, Albert Pike was at all times a striking figure on this 19th century American scene.

He was descended [as was also the famed explorer, Zebulon Pike, who died in 1813] from John Pike, an emigree from Wiltshire, England, to the Massachusetts Bay Colony in 1635. Albert Pike was born in a house on Greene Street, Boston, December 29, 1809 to Benjamin and Sarah Andrews Pike. In the Autumn of 1816 Benjamin Pike moved with his family from Boston to nearby Newburyport. There, when only six years old, Albert Pike saw President James Monroe pass through the town; and when 13 he shook hands with the Marquis de Lafayette when the famous Frenchman visited Newburyport. His father had a difficult time supporting his large family by work on the farm and by his trade as a cobbler. Albert's opportunities at schools in the neighborhood came largely in recognition of his outstanding record as a student. At 15 he was admitted to the Framingham Academy.

Preparing to enter Harvard University, he passed every academic examination required; and while studying for these tests, he was earning money at various jobs and by teaching, in order to accumulate the funds he would need to pay in advance for his first college term. But when he presented himself for admission to Harvard, he was told that he must pay in advance not only for his first term but for the second also before he could be admitted. This was perhaps the first bitter disappointment of his life and he was obliged to put aside any further thought of entering Harvard University.

From 1826 to 1831, from the age of 16 to 21, Albert Pike had been acquiring a substantial reputation in Newburyport as a teacher, essayist and poet. Despite his youth he taught Latin, Greek, Algebra and higher mathematics and opened a school in a room in the Masonic Hall at Newburyport. His poems and essays had been published in *Bower of Taste, Yankee and Boston Literary Gazette, The Essayist,* and *The American Monthly Magazine.*

In March of 1831, at the age of 21, his hope of entering Harvard denied, and looking for new opportunities, he left New England. His assets were a good classical education, intelligence, perception and talent, a zest for life, and great physical well-being. Traveling to Albany, Rochester and Buffalo, he took the stage to Cleveland, Cincinnati and Nashville; thence into Kentucky, and from Paducah he took the river boat to Cairo, Illinois. In July he was on his way up the Mississippi to St. Louis. There he joined a party being formed by Charles Brent, famed trader, on an expedition to Santa Fe. The party moved on to Independence, Missouri, a principal trading center in that time, arriving there in August and setting out for Santa Fe early in September.

For the next three months before Pike reached Taos, New Mexico, the young man from the classrooms of New England discovered that his classical education was of little practical use to him in the primitive life and hardships of the western plains and desert country where he was obliged to join in the hunt for buffalo and game to provide food for survival. It was a rugged experience for a young man of 21 to encounter for the first time, but he survived it without turning back. After reaching Taos in late November [1831] he remained in New

Mexico for the next nine months, moving from place to place. His experiences and observations are described in detail in his *Prose Sketches Written in the Western Country.* Today it frequently goes unnoticed that this work was written by Pike in his twenty-first and twenty-second years. In August [1832] he joined a party into the Commanche Indian country to trap for beaver, and had his first encounters with the "red men" with whom he was to have so much association in later years. Returning from this expedition he arrived at Fort Smith, Arkansas, on December 10, 1832 and nineteen days later marked his twenty-third birthday. In Fort Smith he formed a close friendship with Captain John Rogers, colorful hero of the War of 1812, and was his guest for a number of weeks.

The year of 1833 was one of new beginnings for the 23-year-old Albert Pike. In March, to sustain himself while finishing work on his *Prose Sketches . . .* [which was published the following year] he took a teaching job at Van Buren, Arkansas. At the same time he contributed verse to the *Advocate* newspaper in Little Rock, and then moved to teach at another school at Little Piney, Arkansas. All this time, too, he was taking notice of the turbulent political events in the Territory, and by October he had left Little Piney to work on the *Advocate* and live in Little Rock. His title, "Assistant Editor" in those days meant doing a little of everything of the work done in a newspaper office, from typesetting to writing editorials. In the winter of 1833-1834 Albert Pike began to "read the law" which was the customary procedure of the time, and in August of 1834, the Superior Court of Arkansas Territory gave him a license to practice law. Thus, at the age of 24, he was embarked upon one of the most important phases of his life and work.

By the end of 1834 he was elected assistant secretary to the upper house of the Arkansas Assembly, and at the same time he continued to practice law and to write political and other articles for the *Advocate.*

One day in the courtroom late in 1834 he observed a beautiful brunette who was party to a legal suit being heard, and through the

Judge he sought and obtained introduction to Mary Ann Hamilton. Soon after, at her home a few miles from Little Rock, she became Mrs. Albert Pike and returned with him to the capital.

In January of 1835, Albert Pike purchased the *Advocate* newspaper, and also entered a law partnership. He gave the paper a decided literary character, and it also provided him with a voice in the political scene on such important local matters as the fight for Statehood. Two years later, however, he consolidated the *Advocate* with the *Times* and thereafter retained only a nominal connection with the newspaper so as to devote more time to his law practice.

The extent of Albert Pike's legal practice is apparent in the record that out of 71 cases before the Supreme Court of Arkansas during 1837-1839, he participated in 23; and in the decade between 1837 and 1846 he participated in nearly a third of all the cases before the Court. In 1835 he was on the committee to draw up the charter for the incorporation of Little Rock. In 1836 he was employed to write the notes and index for the revision and codification of the State Statutes; and in 1843 he prepared for publication the first *Arkansas [Legal] Form Book*. His law practice embraced every kind and variety of legal work.

After his marriage he built one of the most handsome homes in Little Rock, situated on an entire square block. He had ten children all of whom were born at Little Rock. Ben Desha Pike, born December 2, 1835, died in February, 1836; Albert Pike, born February 23, 1837 died two days later; Luther Hamilton Pike, born August 20, 1838, survived him; Walter Lacy Pike, born June 29, 1840, died April 6, 1863; Isadore Pike, his eldest daughter, born January 20, 1842, died July 7, 1869; Lilian Pike, born February 22, 1843, survived him and cared for him in his last illness; Albert Holden Pike, born October 4, 1844, was drowned May 16, 1858; Clarence Pike, born in August, 1846, died in February 1848; Eustice Pike, born June 15, 1848, died July 24, 1848; and Yvon Pike, born September 10, 1849 survived him.

Thus it will be seen that from his 25th year in 1835 until his 40th year in 1850 Albert Pike's life was one of intense struggle in the law and politics of Arkansas, marked by recurring personal tragedy within his family, and by occasional travels which gave him small respite. After these 15 crowded years he was to describe himself as being "weary and worn out," and he appeared perhaps subconsciously to be seeking relief from the pressures of his ever accumulating responsibilities in Little Rock.

As early as 1851, in his 41st year, he considered establishing a law practice in New Orleans, specializing in civil law, which he anticipated would be less demanding upon his emotions and energies and give him time for other interests. He resumed the study of French, so necessary in the Louisiana of that day. By early 1855 he was admitted to practice before the Supreme Court and other courts of Louisiana, and had formed a law partnership with Logan Hunton of New Orleans, making his residence there.

But Ann Pike and his family remained in Little Rock, so that his ties and responsibilities in Arkansas were not completely severed. Although his residence in New Orleans was of necessity intermittent, it was both fruitful and significant to his later life. Already a pattern of Masonic activity was developing, to which we will return later. However, in New Orleans Pike did succeed in finding time to indulge his talents as a scholar. As part of his design to practice law in Louisiana he prepared, during 1855, his *Notes on the Civil Code of Louisiana.* In New Orleans he did much of his work on *Maxims of the Roman Law,* completed in 1876, never published but which the late Judge Charles S. Lobingier described as entitling Albert Pike to outstanding distinction in the field of comparative law. During this time he was also reading and studying innumerable French rituals and records, assembling materials for a history of Freemasonry in France, sending copies and suggested revisions to Charleston on Scottish Rite rituals, and serving a term as Grand Master of the Grand Consistory of Louisiana.

Eventually giving up the struggle to remain in New Orleans, in the life he found so congenial there, Albert Pike returned to Arkansas. He served a brief term as an Associate Justice of the Supreme Court of Arkansas, but was soon thereafter involved in the trials and turmoils of the Confederacy—an era of personal rivalries, betrayals, and all the evils of war. The events of those days are so controversial, even now, that it would require a detailed biography to trace Albert Pike through this dark period. Because of earlier military experience, his knowledge of the Indian tribes, and his experiences on the frontier and in the western country, he was commissioned a Brigadier General. The ultimate fate and judgment of Pike's rivals and enemies has served to clarify and enhance his own performance in those days, but so complicated is the picture that it may not be drawn in generalities. Such experiences would have permanently embittered or destroyed a lesser man, but for Albert Pike they became a new strength and not a poison. This was the essence of his greatness. Following the war between the States he was to turn his life and talents as a classical scholar, poet, essayist, pioneer explorer, teacher, lawyer, jurist and soldier into an entirely new work which was to make use of all of his talents—Freemasonry.

ALBERT PIKE, FREEMASON

ALBERT PIKE was raised a Master Mason in Western Star Lodge No. 2, Little Rock, Arkansas, in August of 1850 when he was 40 years of age. That he gave to Masonry the same intense interest he brought to everything he undertook is evident in the record of his activity from the beginning of his Masonic life. Two years after being raised, he became a charter member and the first Worshipful Master of Magnolia Lodge No. 60, Little Rock. On November 7, 1853, at the age of 43, he was named chairman of the Grand Lodge Committee on Masonic Law and Usage, as well as chairman of a committee to revise, collate and digest the Decisions of the Grand Lodge. At the same time he was named chairman of the Grand Lodge Committee on Foreign Correspondence. In the following year he was named chairman of the Grand Lodge Committee on Library, and of a committee to prepare a system of laws and by-laws for the government of subordinate lodges. In November of 1853 he was elected a trustee of St. John's College [established by the Grand Lodge of Arkansas] and was subsequently elected its President. All this within the first three years of his Masonic membership, but it was not all. In November of 1853 he was elected Grand High Priest of the Grand Chapter of Royal Arch Masons of Arkansas, and reelected in 1854, and served virtually the same committees for the Grand Chapter as in the Grand Lodge. In 1852 and 1853 he also received the Cryptic and Templar degrees.

On March 20, 1853, at Charleston, South Carolina, he received the degrees of the Ancient and Accepted Scottish Rite, from the 4th to the 32nd, personally from Albert G. Mackey. Through Masonry the two men had already had close association in the work of Royal Arch General Grand Chapter committees, and a mutual affection and regard was to endure until Mackey's death in 1881. Doubtless it was by Mackey's encouragement that Albert Pike, during his intermittent sojourn in New Orleans, turned his attention to the degree work of the Scottish Rite; and Pike certainly observed, if he did not participate in, the important Concordat concluded at New Orleans in 1855 regularizing the Rite in that area.

When Albert Pike came to the Scottish Rite its entire membership in this country was less than one thousand. Its degrees were fragmentary, its organizational activity desultory, its influence slight. But Pike envisoned what the Rite might be, and he devoted increasing proportions of his time to study and to planning for its future. Elected and receiving the 33° while in New Orleans in 1857, he was elected an Active Member in the following year, and Sovereign Grand Commander on January 3, 1859. He was the eighth of the sixteen Grand Commanders between 1801 and 1957. Following the war he little by little dropped his other work and activities, eventually devoting his time almost exclusively to Freemasonry in general and the Scottish

Rite in particular. Certainly for the last twenty years of his life, Freemasonry occupied most of his time. In his revision of the Scottish Rite rituals he provided a panorama of moral and philosophical thought progressive from degree to degree, a coherent and related series of Masonic lessons. He improved the quality and effectiveness of the Masonic Law of the Rite, embodied in the Supreme Council Statutes. By personally visiting from Valley to Valley and Orient to Orient, he encouraged high standards in the organizational structure of the Rite; and these travels were more often at his own expense, and no little inconvenience. His personality and reputation attracted men of high calibre to lead the work in the different Orients. To lay more firmly and securely the foundations of the Rite, he engaged in exhaustive historical research and published these findings in the *Official Bulletin* [10 volumes]. He waged unceasing attack upon irregular Masonry, notably "Cerneauism." In his correspondence and influence with Masonic leaders abroad he did much to encourage the universality of the Rite. He laid the firm foundations for what is the Southern Jurisdiction of the Ancient and Accepted Scottish Rite today, with its two hundred separate Valleys in the 33 States, the District of Columbia, and U. S. territorial possessions, and its present membership of nearly a half million Scottish Rite Masons.

In his last years he was confined more and more to his rooms in the old House of the Temple, 3rd and E Streets, Northwest, in Washington, D. C., attended with devoted care by his daughter, Lilian. His wife had died at Little Rock, after a long and lingering illness, on April 14, 1876, never having been a part of his Washington life or his travels. Earlier, in 1869 his eldest daughter, Isadore, had died and he wrote at that time "Nobody was so dear to me as Isadore, and nobody loved me as she did . . ." In the last ten years of his life, he formed a warm friendship with Vinnie Ream, the famous sculptress. His many letters to her over this period are filled with recollections of his own lifetime and of his personal philosophy, opinions and conclusions. Perhaps he never wrote to anyone else with such freedom and friendliness and these letters form a valuable record of the man.

ALBERT PIKE

He passed from mortal life at 8 o'clock in the evening on April 2, 1891 in the fourth month of his 81st year. Previous to his death he had said:

> "When I am dead, I wish my monument to be builded only in the hearts and memories of my Brethren of the Ancient and Accepted Scottish Rite, and my name to be remembered by them in every country, no matter what language men speak there, where the light of the Ancient and Accepted Scottish Rite shall shine, and its oracles of truth and wisdom be reverently listened to."

R.B.H.

THE ALBERT PIKE MUSEUM AND ITS SETTING IN THE ARKANSAS OZARKS.

BIBLIOGRAPHY

GENERAL

BIOGRAPHY.

ADDRESS. [At a banquet given in his honor by his friends in Washington, D. C., who had received a false report of his death.] *In* "Life-wake of the fine Arkansas gentleman [Pike] who died before his time," p. 16-24.

AUTOBIOGRAPHY. *In* Hallum, John. Biographical and pictorial history of Arkansas, v. 1, p. 215-221.

Same in Los Angeles Freemason, v. 14, no. 4, January, 1910, p. 104-107; Masonic Journal, Portland. Me., v. 4, no. 7, June. 1891, p. 211-217; New Age Magazine, entitled "The resurrection speech of Albert Pike," v. XI, no. 5, Nov., 1909, p. 459-461; *His* Occasional Bulletins, no. 12, p. 7-12; *His* Official Bulletins, v. 10, p. 409-414.

In the copy of Hallum in the Library of the Supreme Council, there are many corrections in Pike's own hand, and the other references above noted are in accordance with these corrections.

AUTOBIOGRAPHY. *In* Ars Quatuor Coronatorum, v. iv, part 2, pp. 116-157. Masonic Celebrites, no. 3—Albert Pike, by R. F. Gould. [Quotes Pike letters to Gould and others, autobiographical.]

[AUTOBIOGRAPHY.] *See* Manuscripts.

REPLY TO A LIBEL. *In* Voice of Masonry, v. 23, no. XI, Nov. 8, 1885, p. 899-902.

Replying to an article in the Christian Cynosure regarding Pike and the Indians.

BATES, JAMES W. By General Albert Pike. *In* Hallum, John. Biographical and pictorial history of Arkansas, v. 1, p. 85-86.

CRITTENDEN, ROBERT. By General Albert Pike. *In* Hallum, John. Biographical and pictorial history of Arkansas, v. 1, p. 65-67.

CROSS, EDWARD. By General Albert Pike. *In* Hallum, John. Biographical and pictorial history of Arkansas, v. 1, p. 80-81.

CUMMINS, WILLIAM. By General Albert Pike. *In* Hallum, John. Biographical and pictorial history of Arkansas, v. 1, p. 82-85.

FARRELLY, TERRENCE. By General Albert Pike. *In* Hallum, John. Biographical and pictorial history of Arkansas, v. 1, p. 87-88.

HALL, SAMUEL S. By General Albert Pike. *In* Hallum, John. Biographical and pictorial history of Arkansas, v. 1, p. 67-70.

HUBBARD, THOMAS. By General Albert Pike. *In* Hallum, John. Biographical and pictorial history of Arkansas, v. 1, p. 88-89.

ISADORE. In memoriam. Isadore. [By Albert Pike.] [N. p. 1869.] [3] p. 8°.

LACY, THOMAS J. By General Albert Pike. *In* Hallum, John. Biographical and pictorial history of Arkansas, v. 1, p. 78-80.

TAYLOR, JOHN. By General Albert Pike. *In* Hallum, John. Biographical and pictorial history of Arkansas, v. 1, p. 70-72.

[THURSTON, DR.] Albert Pike's touching letter to a dying friend. (From the Fort Smith [Arkansas] Tribune.) Washington, September 3, 1885. [3] p. 8°.

Same in Builder, The. v. 3, no. 10, Oct., 1917, p. 304; New Age Magazine, v. 14, no. 3, March, 1911, p. 301.

WALKER, DAVID. By General Albert Pike. *In* Hallum, John. Biographical and pictorial history of Arkansas, v. 1, p. 81-82.

YELL, ARCHIBALD. By General Albert Pike. *In* Hallum, John. Biographical and pictorial history of Arkansas, v. 1, p. 86-87.

LANGUAGE.

ANCIENT ALPHABETS. *See* Manuscripts.

BOOK OF THE WORDS. *See* Masonic.

TRANSLATIONS OF THE RIG VEDA. *See* Manuscripts.

VOCABULARIES OF INDIAN LANGUAGES. *See* Manuscripts.

VOCABULARIES OF SANSCRIT WORDS. *See* Manuscripts.

LAW.

Anecdotes of the Arkansas Bar. By a backwoods lawyer. [Albert Pike.] *In* Porter, William T. The big bear of Arkansas, and other sketches, p. 159-163.

The Arkansas Form Book, containing a large variety of legal forms and instruments, adapted to popular wants and professional use, in the State of Arkansas, with a summary of the principles of law, of most ordinary application. By Albert Pike, Counsellor at law. Little Rock, William E. Woodruff, 1842. 4+425 pp. 8vo.

Arkansas. Supreme Court. Opinion of the Supreme Court of Arkansas in the State vs. Samuel W. Williams, At. Gen., on Quo Warranto, delivered August 8, 1864. Washington, Arkansas: [Opinion delivered by Justice Albert Pike] 94 p., 1 p. of errata. 8°

Copy in Harvard Law Library.

A legal right unrighteously exercised. *In his* Occasional Bulletins, No. 11, p. 3-5.

Same in Masonic Review, v. 75, no. 2, March, 1891, p. 107-110.

Relates to what Pike terms the sharp practice of a book concern in New York, in connection with the copyright law.

Maxims of the Roman law. *See* Manuscripts.

Notes on the civil code of Louisiana. *See* Manuscripts.

Reports of cases argued and determined in the Supreme Court of law and equity of the State of Arkansas. [January term, 1837 to July term, 1844] 5v. 8°.

- v. 1. Albert Pike, reporter. Little Rock, printed by Budd and Colby, 1840. 655p.
- v. 2. By Albert Pike, counselor at law. Little Rock, published by George H. Burnett, 1841. 639 p.
- v. 3. By Albert Pike, counselor at law. Little Rock, published by Wm. E. Woodruff, 1842. 624 p.
- v. 4. By Albert Pike, counselor at law. Little Rock, published by B. J. Borden, 1843. 668 p.
- v. 5. By Albert Pike, counselor at law. Little Rock, published by B. J. Borden, 1845. 769 p.

Same [Reprint] Press of Tunnah & Pittard, Little Rock, 1905-1906. 5v. 8°.

Revised statutes of the state of Arkansas adopted at the October session of the General Assembly of said state, A. D. 1837, in the year of our independence the sixty-second and of the state, the second year. Revised by William McK. Ball and Sam C. Roane. Notes and index by Albert Pike. Boston, Weeks, Jordan & Company, publishers, 1838. 15+956 p. 8°.

Rules and orders of the Supreme Court. *See* Manuscripts.

B I B L I O G R A P H Y

The Superior Court [of Arkansas.] By General Albert Pike. *In* Hallum, John. Biographical and pictorial history of Arkansas, v. 1, p. 72-78.

Reminiscent of judges and lawyers of the early days in Arkansas.

Abrahams, James vs. John Wilkins. In the Supreme Court of Arkansas. No................, July term, 1853. Appeal from Lafayette circuit court. Printed by Stillwell & Wassell, Little Rock, Ark. 23 p. 8°.

Signed: Pike & Cummins, counsel for appellee.

Anthony, Mark S. vs. The heirs of Letitia Neill. In the Supreme Court of Arkansas. No................, July term, 1851. Appeal from Pulaski circuit court. Printed by John M. Butler, Little Rock. 105 p. 8°.

Signed: Pike & Cummins.

Arkansas, State of vs. The President & Directors of the Bank of Washington. In the Supreme Court of Arkansas. Printed by Stillwell & Wassell, Little Rock, Ark. [N. d., *after* 1844.] 17p. 8°.

Signed: Pike & Cummins, counsel for appellees.

Ashley, Mary W. W. et al. vs. Robert Cunningham, et al. and Robert Cunningham, et al. vs. Mary W. W. Ashley, et al. In the Supreme Court of Arkansas, No................, July term, 1854. On cross appeal: From Pulaski Circuit court, in chancery. Printed by Stillwell & Wassell, Little Rock, Ark. 40p. 8°.

Signed: Pike & Cummins, counsel for Cunningham's heirs.

The Autocrat vs. The Magnolia. Supreme Court of the United States. No. 80, December term, 1855. Brief for the appellants. Gideon, printer, 511 9th street, Washington, D. C. 24p. 8°.

Signed: Albert Pike, counsel for the libellants.

Avery, William T., plaintiff in error vs. The United States of America, defendants in error. Supreme Court of the United States. No. 170. Additional suggestions in behalf of plaintiff in error. Albert Pike, Robert W. Johnson, of counsel. [N. p. N. d.] 14 p. 8°.

Bank of the State of Arkansas vs. W. H. Etter. In the Supreme Court of Arkansas. No................, July term, 1853. Appeal from Hempstead circuit court. Printed by Stillwell & Wassell, Little Rock, Ark. 6p. 8°.

Signed: Pike & Cummins, solicitors.

Bank of Washington, President and Directors of the, and James Holford's administrators. plaintiffs vs. The State of Arkansas, defendants. Supreme Court of the United States, December term, 1856. Error to the Supreme Court of Arkansas. Argument for plaintiffs in error. Gideon, printer, 511 9th street, Washington, D. C. 51p. 8°.

Signed: Albert Pike, counsel for plaintiffs in error.

BANK OF WASHINGTON, THE PRESIDENT AND DIRECTORS OF THE, AND JAMES HOLFORD'S ADMINISTRATORS, PLAINTIFFS VS. THE STATE OF ARKANSAS AND THE TRUSTEES OF THE REAL ESTATE BANK OF THE STATE OF ARKANSAS, DEFENDANTS. Supreme Court of the United States, December term, 1856. Error to the Supreme Court of Arkansas. Argument for the plaintiffs in error. Gideon, printer, 511 9th street, Washington, D. C. 27p. 8°.

Signed: Albert Pike, of counsel for the appellants.

BANK OF WASHINGTON, THE PRESIDENT AND DIRECTORS OF THE, AND JAMES HOLFORD'S ADMINISTRATORS, APPELLANTS VS. APPEAL FROM THE CHANCERY COURT OF PULASKI CO. THE STATE OF ARKANSAS, AND THE TRUSTEES OF THE REAL ESTATE BANK OF THE STATE OF ARKANSAS, APPELLEES. In the Supreme Court of Arkansas, July term, A. D. 1855. [N. p. N. d.] 30p. 8°.

Signed: Pike & Cummins, of counsel for the appellants.

BANK OF WASHINGTON, THE PRESIDENT AND DIRECTORS OF, ET AL., APPELLANTS VS. APPEAL FROM THE CHANCERY COURT OF PULASKI. The State of Arkansas, and the Bank of the State of Arkansas, appellees. In the Supreme Court of Arkansas, at July term, A. D. 1855. [N. p. N. d.] 53p. 8°.

Signed: Pike & Cummins, attorneys for the appellants. In the copy before us "Pike & Cummins" is ruled out and "Albert Pike" substituted in his own hand.

BARNARD, THOMAS, THE HEIRS OF VS. SILAS CRAIG AND THE EXECUTRIX AND HEIRS OF CHESTER ASHLEY. Supreme Court of the United States. December term, 1853. Appeal from the circuit court of the United States for the Eastern District of Arkansas. Argument for the appellants. Gideon, print. [Washington, D. C.] 41p. 8°.

Signed: Albert Pike, counsel for Barnard's heirs.

BAUMAN, WALBERGA VS. DAVID BAUMAN. In the Supreme Court of Arkansas. No................, July term, 1854. Appeal from Pulaski circuit court. Printed at the True Democrat office. 9p. 8°.

Signed: Pike & Cummins, sol's.

BEEBE, BOSWELL, AND OTHERS, APPELLANTS VS. WILLIAM RUSSELL, APPELLEE. Supreme Court of the United States, December term, 1856. Appeal from the circuit court for the Eastern District of Arkansas, in chancery. Argument for the appellee. Gideon, printer, 511 Ninth street, Washington, D. C. 46p. 8°.

Signed: Albert Pike, counsel for William Russell.

BISCOE, HENRY L., ET AL. VS. RICHARD C. BYRD, ET AL. In the Supreme Court of Arkansas. No................, July term, 1853. Appeal from Pulaski circuit Court, in chancery. Printed by Stillwell & Wassell, Little Rock, Ark. 26p. 8°.

Signed: Pike & Cummins, counsel for complainants.

BISCOE, HENRY L., AND OTHERS, APPELLANTS VS. DAVID R. COULTER AND TURNER H. BUCKNER, APPELLEES. In the Supreme Court of Arkansas. No................, July term, 1854. Appeal from Sevier circuit court in chancery. Printed by Stillwell & Wassell, Little Rock, Ark. 21p. 8°.

Signed: Pike & Cummins, counsel for the trustees.

B I B L I O G R A P H Y

Biscoe, H. L., et al. vs. Rob't H. Scott & Grandison D. Royston. In the Supreme Court of Arkansas. No................., January term, 1854. Appeal from Hempstead circuit court. Printed by Stillwell & Wassell, Little Rock, Ark. 14p. 8°.

Signed: Pike & Cummins, counsel for appellants.

Biscoe H. L., et al., trustees R. E. Bank vs. Wood Tucker, et al. In the Supreme Court of Arkansas. No................., July term, 1851. Printed by John M. Butler, Little Rock, Ark. 36p. 8°.

Signed: Albert Pike, solicitor for appellant.

Bizzell, William H. vs. Paul R. Hooker, et al. In the Supreme Court of Arkansas. No................., July term, 1853. Appeal from Hempstead circuit court. Printed by Stillwell & Wassell, Little Rock, Ark. 9p. 8°.

Signed: Pike & Cummins, attorneys.

Burk, Patrick, appl't vs. William H. Gaines, et al., appellees. In the Supreme Court of Arkansas. No................., July term, 1854. Appeal from Hot Springs circuit court. Stillwell & Wassell, printers, Little Rock, Ark. 22p. 8°.

Signed: Pike & Cummins, counsel for Burk.

Carter, Landon D., et al. vs. Stephan Cantrell. In the Supreme Court of Arkansas. No................., July term, 1853. Appeal from Jefferson circuit court in chancery. Printed by Stillwell & Wassell, Little Rock, Ark. 21p. 8°.

Signed: Pike & Cummins, counsel for complainants.

The Choctaw nation of indians vs. the United States. In the United States Court of Claims, December term, 1883. No. 12,742. Argument for the Claimant. James W. Denver, of counsel for himself and the original counsel of the Choctaw nation. Judd & Detweiler, printers, [Washington,] 25p. 8°.

In the copy in the Library of the Supreme Council at Washington is noted on the title page in Pike's own hand: "Written by Albert Pike."

The Choctaw nation of indians vs. the United States. Argument for the claimant. In the [Supreme Court of the] United States, [October] term, 188[6] [Washington]. Judd & Detweiler, printers. 25p. 8°.

Albert Pike and James W. Denver, of counsel. The printed title or heading was: "In the United States Court of Claims, December term, 1883." The words in brackets were written in by Pike, after crossing out the portions necessary to form the title for his new brief.

Choctaw nation of indians. Memorial of P. P. Pitchlynn, delegate of Choctaw nation of indians, upon the right of that nation to be paid the moneys awarded to it by the United States Senate, on the 9th day of March, A. D. 1859. House of Representatives, 43d congress, 1st session. Mis. Doc. No. 89. January 21, 1874. 46p. 8°.

Written by Albert Pike.

Choctaw nation of indians. Testimony of Albert Pike. In the Senate of the United States, 49th congress, 2nd session. Report No. 1978, February 28, 1887, p. 33-56. Report to accompany Senate resolution of December 14, 1886, directing an inquiry to be made concerning claims of professional, or other services made upon the Choctaw nation on account of certain judgments rendered against the United States.

Choctaw nation of indians. To the Senators and Representatives of the United States. 7p. 8°. Caption title.

Signed: Albert Pike, counsellor at law, Washington, January 31, 1877. Refuting the denunciation by a public journal, laid on the desks of members of the House.

Clark, Hulda, et al, apps. vs. Jesse Shelton, appellee. In the Supreme Court of Arkansas. No................., July term, 1853. Printed by Stillwell & Wassell, Little Rock, Ark. 15p. 8°.

Signed: Albert Pike, counsel for appellee.

Cockrill, John vs. Franklin S. Warner. In the Supreme Court of Arkansas. No................., January term, 1853. On appeal from Lafayette circuit court, in chancery. Printed by John M. Butler, Little Rock, Ark. 31p. 8°.

Signed: Pike & Cummins.

Cornelius, Jester, appellant, in the matter of the will of William Cornelius. In the Supreme Court of Arkansas. No................., January term, 1853. Appeal from Hempstead circuit court. Printed by Stillwell & Wassell, [Little Rock, Ark.] 7p. 8°.

Signed: Pike & Cummins.

Cornelius, Jester, appellant, in the matter of the will of William Cornelius. In the Supreme Court of Arkansas. No................., January term, 1854. Appeal from Hempstead circuit court. 7p. 8°.

Signed: Pike & Cummins.

Cox vs. McPherson. Supreme Court of the District of Columbia. No. 3,268, in equity. Brief for plaintiff. [Washington, about 1873?] 15p. 8°.

Signed: Albert Pike, Robert W. Johnson, L. H. Pike, of counsel for the plaintiff.

Craig, Junius W., The creditors of the estate of, deceased, and Carlton, administrator of the estate of Lewis E. Craig, legatee vs. Emma J. Wright, executrix of the last will of Junius W. Craig. In the Supreme Court of Arkansas. Argument for the appellee. Albert Pike, Charles W. Adams, L. H. Pike [of counsel] for Emma J. Wright. [N. P. about 1867?] 43p. 8°.

Crittenden, Ann Innes vs. Matilda Johnson and others. In the Supreme Court of Arkansas. No................., January term, 1853. Appeal from Pulaski circuit court, in chancery. Printed by Stillwell & Wassell, Little Rock, Ark. 24p. 8°.

Signed: Pike & Cummins, counsel for appellant.

Culbertson vs. The Southern Belle. Supreme Court of the United States. No. 98, December term, 1855. Argument for the appellees. Gideon, printer, 511 Ninth street, Washington, D. C. 11p. 8°.

Signed: Albert Pike, proctor and advocate for the appellees.

Cunningham, Matthew, Heirs of vs. Roswell Beebe, Mary W. W. Ashley, et al. In the Supreme Court of Arkansas. January term, 1855. Case

No................. Appeal from Pulaski circuit court. Stillwell & Wassell, printers, Little Rock, Ark. 18p. 8°.

Signed: Pike & Cummins, counsel for Cunningham's heirs.

CUNNINGHAM, MATTHEW, HEIRS OF VS. ROSWELL BEEBE, AND HEIRS OF CHESTER ASHLEY. In the Supreme Court of Arkansas, July term, 1855. Response to petition for reconsideration. Printed by J. M. & J. D. Butler, Little Rock, Ark. 82p. 8°.

Signed: Pike & Cummins, solicitors for heirs of Cunningham.

CURRAN, JAMES M., PLAINTIFF IN ERROR VS. THE STATE OF ARKANSAS, AND THE BANK OF THE STATE OF ARKANSAS, DEFENDANTS IN ERROR. Supreme Court of the United States, December term, 1851. Argument in behalf of plaintiff in error. 39p. 8°.

Signed: Albert Pike, solicitor for plaintiff in error.

CURRY, A. P. EX PARTE PETITION FOR SUPERSEDEAS. In the Supreme Court of Tennessee. Knoxville. Argument in opposition to the petition. Chas W. Adams, L. V. Dixon, L. H. Pike and Albert Pike. [1869.] 14p. 8°.

DAVIES, MILDRED P., ADMINISTRATRIX OF THE ESTATE AND WIDOW OF ANTHONY H. DAVIES AND HIS HEIRS-AT-LAW, FOR THEMSELVES AND FOR THE CREDITORS OF SAID ESTATE VS. ABNER L. GAINES. In the Chicot circuit court. In chancery. Albert Pike, of counsel for complainant. Cunningham & McIntosh, printers, 930 Pennsylvania avenue, [Washington, about 1871.] 79p. 8°.

DENVER, JAMES L. AND CHARLES F. PECK, APPELLANTS VS. ARCHIBALD ROANE, EXECUTOR OF THE TESTAMENT OF JAMES HUGHES, DEC'D. Supreme Court of the United States, October term, 1878. No. 240. On appeal from the Supreme Court of the District of Columbia. Brief and argument for appellants. Pike & Johnson, of counsel. [Washington, D. C. Judd & Detweiler, printers, 1878.] 162p. 8°. Cover title.

DICKSON, JOHN VS. LOUISA C. RICHARDSON, ADMR'X OF HENRY RICHARDSON. In the Supreme Court of Arkansas. No................., July term, 1853. Appeal from Lafayette circuit court, in chancery. Printed by Stillwell & Wassell, Little Rock, Ark. 18p. 8°.

Signed: Pike & Cummins, counsel for Dickson.

DILLARD, JOHN, AD. VS. CONSTANTA WILSON. In the Supreme Court of Arkansas. No................., January term, 1853. Appeal from Crawford circuit court, in chancery. Printed by John M. Butler, Little Rock, Ark. 16p. 8°.

Signed: Pike & Cummins.

DYER, CATHERINE, ET AL. VS. MARK AND JOAB BEAN. In the Supreme Court of Arkansas. No................., July term, 1854. Appeal from Franklin circuit court, in chancery. Stillwell & Wassell, printers, Little Rock, Ark. 8p. 8°.

Signed: Pike & Cummins, counsel for appellees.

FARRELLY, TERENCE, EDWARD C. MORTON, ET AL., HEIRS AND REPRESENTATIVES OF FREDERIC NOTREBE, APPELLANTS VS. WILLIAM W. WOODFOLK, APPELLEE. In the Supreme Court of the United States. Appeal from the circuit court of the

United States for the Eastern District of Arkansas. Argument for the appellants. [N. p. about 1853.] 41p. 8°.

Signed: Albert Pike, counsel for appellants.

FARRINGTON, WILLIAM M., PLAINTIFF IN ERROR VS. ROLFE S. SAUNDERS. COLLECTOR OF INTERNAL REVENUE, DEFENDANT. In the Supreme Court of the United States. December term, 1868. Argument for the plaintiff in error. Albert Pike, Robert W. Johnson [of counsel for Farrington.] [N. p., about 1868?] 66p. 8°.

FIRST NATIONAL BANK OF LOUISVILLE VS. THE COMMONWEALTH OF KENTUCKY. No. 301. In the Supreme Court of the United States. Error to court of appeals of Kentucky. Argument for defendant in error. Albert Pike, Robert W. Johnson, of counsel. [N. p., about 1868?] 48+1p. 8°.

FOWLKES, EDW. D., ADM'TRS OF, APPELLANTS VS. JOANNA T. CARRINGTON AND OTHERS, APPELLEES. In the Supreme Court of Arkansas. No................., July term, 1854. Appeal from Hempstead circuit court in chancery. Printed by Stillwell & Wassell, Little Rock, Ark. 19p. 8°.

Signed: Pike & Cummins, counsel for E. B. Fowlkes.

GARLAND, JOSIAH, PLAINTIFF IN ERROR VS. WILLIAM WYNN, DEFENDANT IN ERROR. In the Supreme Court of the United States. No................., December term, 1855. Error to the Supreme Court of Arkansas. Argument for defendant in error. John Wassell, printer, Little Rock, Ark. 102p. 8°.

Signed: Albert Pike, counsel for Wynn.

GREENWALD AND OTHERS VS. BOND. In the Supreme Court of the United States. Term of 1876-1877. No. 68. Supplemental brief for plaintiff in error [Washington.] 10p. 8°.

Signed: Albert Pike, Robert W. Johnson, Luther H. Pike, of counsel.

GREENWOOD & MORRIS, PLAINTIFFS AND APPELLEES VS. THE HOME MUTUAL INSURANCE CO., OF NEW ORLEANS, DEFENDANT AND APPELLANT. In the Supreme Court of Louisiana. No. 3724. Argument for appellant. [New Orleans? about 1854?] 40p. 8°.

Signed: Hunton & Pike, counsel for appellants.

HALLIDAY, WILLIAM P., AND OTHERS PLAINTIFFS IN ERROR VS. THOMAS A. HAMILTON, AND ANOTHER, DEFENDANTS IN ERROR. Supreme Court of the United States. Argument for plaintiffs in error. Albert Pike, Robert W. Johnson, of counsel. [N. p., about 1867?] 47p. 8°.

HEMPHILL, ANDREW VS. W. L. MILLER. In the Supreme Court of Arkansas. No................., July term, 1852. Appeal from Lafayette circuit court in chancery.. Printed by John M. Butler, Little Rock, Ark. 35p. 8°.

Signed: Pike & Cummins.

HEMPSTEAD, B. F., LAND AGENT, &C., APPELLANT VS. THE ADS. AND HEIRS OF G. W. UNDERHILL, DEC'D, APPELLEES. In the Supreme Court of Arkansas. July term, 1856. Appeal from Hempstead circuit court. Printed by James D. Butler. Little Rock, Ark. 32p. 8°.

Signed: Albert Pike, counsel for the appellees.

HILL, EZRA, ET AL. VS. BENJ. F. CAWTHON, ET AL. In the Supreme Court of Arkansas. No................, July term, 1853. Appeal from Ouachita circuit court. Printed by Stillwell & Wassell, Little Rock, Ark. 4p. 8°.
Signed: Pike & Cummins, counsel for appellants.

HOT SPRINGS OF ARKANSAS, Argument as to the title to the, on behalf of the New Madrid location of Francis Langlois. [N. P., about 1852?] 13p. 8°.
Signed: Albert Pike, attorney for Henry M. Rector.

HOT SPRINGS OF ARKANSAS, Argument as to the title to the, on behalf of the New Madrid location of Francis Langlois. Gideon, printer, [Washington, D. C., about 1852.] 19p. 8°.
Signed: Albert Pike, attorney for Henry M. Rector.

THE HOT SPRINGS CASES. George McKay and William W. Gitt, vs. The United States, Henry M. Rector, and others. Supreme Court of the United States. Term of 1875-76. No................. Brief for Henry M. Rector. Albert Pike, Robert W. Johnson, John B. Sanborn, Charles King, of counsel for Rector. [Washington, D. C.] 20p. 8°.

THE HOT SPRINGS CASES. William H. Gaines and others vs. the United States, Henry M. Rector, and others. Supreme Court of the United States. Term of 1875-76. No. 772. Brief for Rector, in opposition to Belding's heirs. Albert Pike, Robert W. Johnson, John B. Sanborn, Charles King, of counsel for Rector. [Washington, D. C.] 26p. 8°.

HUTT, WILLIAM S. AND JAS. T. STARK, APPELLEES, ADS. THOMAS D. MERRICK AND JOSEPH FENNO, APPELLANTS. In the Supreme Court of Arkansas. No................, July term, 1854. Appeal from Pulaski circuit court in chancery. Stillwell & Wassell, printers, Little Rock, Ark. 12p. 8°.
Signed: Trapnall and Pike & Cummins, counsel for appellants.

JACKSON, ISAAC N. VS. BOB, A SLAVE. In the Supreme Court of Arkansas. No. ...., July term, 1854. Appeal from Sevier circuit court. Printed at the True Democrat Office, [Little Rock, Ark.] 22p. 8°.
Signed: Pike & Cummins, attorneys for plaintiff.

JONES, ISAAC N., APPELLANT VS. WM. JAS. MC LEAN, SURV'G PARTNER, AND JOHN M. BASS, ET AL., EX'RS OF HARRY R. W. HILL, DECEASED, APPELLANTS, AND THE SAME ADS. THE SAME, ON CROSS APPEAL. In the Supreme Court of Arkansas. No................, January term, 1854. From Lafayette circuit court, in chancery. Stillwell & Wassell, printers, Little Rock, Ark. 52p. 8°.
Signed: Pike & Cummins, counsel for Hill and others.

JONES, STEPHEN M., APPELLANT VS. JOSEPH I. ANDREWS, PINCKNEY REED AND H. W. BRYSON, APPELLEES. Supreme Court of the United States. No. 221. From the circuit court of the United States for the district of West Tennessee. Argument for the appellees. Albert Pike, Robert W. Johnson, of counsel. [N. p., about 1866?] 25p. 8°.

LAWSON, JAS. & L. CHASE, APPELLEES, ADVS. THE BANK OF THE STATE OF ARKANSAS, APPELLANT. In the Supreme Court of Arkansas. No................, January term, 1854. Appeal from Pulaski circuit court. Printed by Stillwell & Wassell, [Little Rock, Ark.] 4p. 8°.

Signed: Pike & Cummins.

McCARRON, THOMAS, APPELLANT VS. THOS. CASSIDY, APPELLEE. In the Supreme Court of Arkansas, July term, 1855. Appeal from Sebastian circuit court in chancery. Printed by J. D. Butler, Little Rock, Ark. 22p. 8°.

Signed: Pike & Cummins for the appellee.

McPHERSON, vs. Cox. On motion for new trial. [Washington? about 1873?] 14p. 8°.

Signed: Albert Pike, L. H. Pike, of counsel for defendant.

McPHERSON, JOHN D., APPELLANT VS. MARY A. COX. In the Supreme Court of the United States. At the term of 1877-78. No. 199. Brief of appellee. [Washington, D. C.] 112p. 8°.

Signed: Albert Pike, Robert W. Johnson, L. H. Pike, of counsel for the appellee.

MARSHALL AND WIFE, ET AL. VS. HEWES SCULL, ET AL. In the Supreme Court of Arkansas. No. ...., January term, 1854. Appeal from the Jefferson circuit court. Printed by Stillwell & Wassell, Little Rock, Ark. 14p. 8°.

Signed: Pike & Cummins, counsel for defendants.

MIMMACK, BERNARD P. VS. THE UNITED STATES OF AMERICA. Supreme Court of the United States. Term of 1878-1879. No. 73. Appeal from the Court of Claims. [Washington, D. C.] 26p. 8°.

Signed: Albert Pike, Luther H. Pike, of counsel.

MOORE & GAIL, ADMS. OF IRWIN VS. G. BLACKMORE, ET AL. In the Supreme Court of Arkansas. No................, July term, 1853. Appeal from Phillips circuit court. Printed by Stilwell & Wassell, Little Rock, Ark. 9p. 8°

Signed: Pike & Cummins, solicitors.

MUSCOGEE OR CREEK NATION OF INDIANS, Memorial of, to the Congress of the United States. [N. p., about 1852?] 24p. 8°.

Signed: Albert Pike, attorney of the Creek nation.

NEWMAN, MARY JANE VS. HORACE B. ALLIS. In the Supreme Court of Arkansas. No................, July term, 1853. Appeal from Pulaski circuit court. Printed by Stillwell & Wassell, Little Rock, Ark. 11p. 8°.

Signed: Pike & Cummins and P. Trapnall, attornies.

On the question Damni et interesse; on the question of domicil. N. p. N. d.

Signed: "Albert Pike, Robert W. Johnson, of counsel for claimants." Pp. 19-32 of a legal case, the particulars of which are not now obtainable.

PATTERSON, E. G., PLAINTIFF IN ERROR VS. THE COMMONWEALTH OF KENTUCKY. In the Supreme Court of the United States. Term of 1878-1879. No. 117. Brief of defendant in error. Albert Pike, Robert W. Johnson, Luther H. Pike, of counsel. Washington, Jos. L. Pearson, printer, 1878. 7p. 8°.

PETTIT & FORD VS. ABNER JOHNSON, ET AL. In the Supreme Court of Arkansas. No................, January term, 1854. Appeal from Chicot circuit court. Printed by Stillwell & Wassell, Little Rock, Ark. 11p. 8°.

Signed: Albert Pike, counsel for Pettit & Ford.

PHELPS, CALVIN VS. JOHN HENRY, ET AL. In the Supreme Court of Arkansas. No................, January term, 1853. On appeal from Crawford circuit court, in chancery. Printed by John M. Butler, Little Rock, Ark. 19p. 8°.

Signed: Pike & Cummins.

PHILLIPS, JAMES, APPELLEE VS. THE ST. LOUIS PERPETUAL INSURANCE CO., APPELLANT. In the Supreme Court of Louisiana. Argument for the appellant. J. B. Steel, print., 60 Camp st. [New Orleans? about 1854?] 28p. 8°.

Signed: Hunton & Pike, counsel for appellants.

PILLOW, JEROME B., PLAINTIFF IN ERROR VS. TRUMAN ROBERTS, DEFENDANT IN ERROR. Supreme Court of the United States. December term, 1851. In error from the circuit court for the Eastern District of Arkansas. [N. p. N. d.] 61p. 8°.

Signed: Albert Pike, attorney for plaintiff in error.

RECTOR, ELIAS VS. A. MOREHOUSE. In the Supreme Court of Arkansas. No..............., July term, 1854. Appeal from Pulaski circuit court. Printed at the True Democrat Office, [Little Rock, Ark.] 9p. 8°.

Signed: Pike & Cummins, attorneys for plaintiff.

RECTOR, HENRY M. VS. THE UNITED STATES AND OTHERS. Supreme Court of the United States. No. 646. Argument upon the claim under the New Madrid location. For the claimant, Rector, Pike & Johnson, Canborn & King, of counsel for Henry M. Rector. [N. p. N. d.] 176p. 8°.

RECTOR, HENRY M., APPELLANT VS. THE UNITED STATES AND OTHERS. Supreme Court of the United States. Term of 1875-6. No. 646. Brief for appellant. Albert Pike, Robert W. Johnson, John B. Sanborn, Charles King, of counsel for Rector. [Washington, D. C.] 70p. 8°.

RINGGOLD VS. PATTERSON. In the Supreme Court of Arkansas. No................, January term, 1854. Appeal from Independence circuit court. Printed by Stillwell & Wassell, [Little Rock, Ark.] 25p. 8°.

Signed: Pike & Cummins & W. Byers, attorneys.

ROANE, JULIA, EXECUTRIX VS. ANN E. RIVERS, COMPLAINANT. In the Supreme Conurt of Arkansas. No. 176. January term, 1854. Appeal from Jefferson, in chancery. Printed by Stillwell & Wassell, [Little Rock, Ark.] 12p. 8°.

Signed: Curran & Gallagher and Pike & Cummins.

ROBERTS, JOSEPH, APPELLANT VS. WILLIAM TOTTEN, APPELLEE. Supreme Court of Arkansas, January term, 1852. On appeal from the circuit court of Pulaski county. Appellee's argument, on petition for reconsideration. [Printed at the office of the Arkansas Whig, Little Rock, Ark.] 14p. 8°.

Signed: Pike & Cummins.

RUSSELL, WILLIAM VS. BUCHANAN & CADY. In the Supreme Court of Arkansas. No................, July term, 1853. Appeal from Pulaski circuit court. Printed by Stillwell & Wassell, Little Rock, Ark. 4p. 8°.

Signed: Pike & Cummins, counsel for appellant.

RYBURN, BENJ. F. VS. EDWARD L. PRYOR. In the Supreme Court of Arkansas. No................, January term, 1853. Appeal from Hempstead circuit court. Printed by John M. Butler, Little Rock, Ark. 23p. 8°.

Signed: Albert Pike, attorney for appellee.

SESSIONS, RICHARD R., DANIEL A. SESSIONS AND SANFORD C. FAULKNER, APPELLANTS VS. JOHN M. PINTARD, APPELLEE. On appeal. In the Supreme Court of the United States, at December term, 1854. From the circuit court of the United States for the Eastern District of Arkansas. Printed by Stillwell & Wassell, Little Rock, Ark. 8p. 8°.

Signed: Albert Pike, counsel for appellants.

SULLIVAN, LEE, VS. JAMES HADLEY, ET AL. In the Supreme Court of Arkansas. No................, January term, 1854. Printed by Stillwell & Wassell [Little Rock, Ark.] 8p. 8°.

Signed: Pike & Cummins.

TAYLOR, FREDERIC, DEC'D, PRE-EMPTION CLAIM OF. Argument for the claim. [N. p., about 1846?] 7p. 8°.

Signed: Albert Pike, att'y for Taylor's administrator.

[TENNESSEE, LEGISLATURE OF, VS. CITIZENS OF.] In the Supreme Court of the United States. .... Term, A. D. 18......... Argument for......... Albert Pike, Robert W. Johnson, advocates. 68p. 8°.

TEXAS, STATE OF, COMPLAINANT VS. GEORGE W. WHITE, JOHN CHILES, AND OTHERS, DEFENDANT. Original suit: No. 6. In the Supreme Court of the United States, December term, 1868. In equity. Argument for John Chiles, defendant. By Albert Pike and Robert W. Johnson, and James Hughes, Esqs. [Washington, D. C.] 96p. 8°.

In the copy in the Library of the Supreme Council at Washington, is the following in Pike's own hand: "Prepared for James Hughes without charge, out of professional courtesy. Albert Pike."

THORN, THOMAS, IN RE THE CREDITORS OF. Bill of the trustees of the Real Estate Bank. In the Supreme Court of Arkansas. No................, July term, 1853. Printed by Stillwell & Wassell, Little Rock, Ark. 19p. 8°.

Signed: Albert Pike, counsel for trustees R. E. Bank.

TODD, WILLIAM H., AS ASSIGNEE OF THE CLAIM OF A. D. KELLY & CO., AND CREDITOR OF THE SUCCESSION OF JUNIUS W. CRAIG, DECEASED VS. JOSEPH S. WOODFOLK, LUCY D. WOODFOLK, AND OTHERS, CLAIMING WITH HIMSELF, CREDITORS OF THE SUCCESSION OF JUNIUS W. CRAIG, DECEASED. In the chancery court of Louisville, State of Kentucky. Upon the marshalling of the assets in Kentucky. Argument of Albert Pike, of counsel for William H. Todd. [N. p., about 1861?] 19p. 8°.

B I B L I O G R A P H Y

TUCKER, PHILIP C., AND ROBERT PULSFORD, APPELLANTS VS. N. A. COWDREY, THE GALVESTON, HOUSTON AND HENDERSON RAILROAD COMPANY, AND OTHERS, APPELLEES. Supreme Court, U. S. Term of 1870-71. No. 212, included in No. 119. Argument for appellants. Albert Pike, Robert W. Johnson, of counsel for appellants. [Washington, D. C.] 79p. 8°.

THE UNITED STATES VS. JAMES L. DAWSON. Supreme Court of the United States, December term, 1853. On certificate of division of opinion from the circuit court of the Eastern District of Arkansas. Gideon, print. [Washington, D. C.] 18p. 8°.

Signed: Albert Pike, counsel for James L. Dawson.

VERY, MARTIN, APPELLANT VS. JONAS LEVY, APPELLEE. Supreme Court of the United States, December term, 1851. No. 130. Appeal from the circuit court for the State of Arkansas. Argument for the appellee. [Little Rock, Ark., 1852.] 15p. 8°.

Signed: Albert Pike, solicitor for the appellee.

WALKER, DAVID, ET AL. VS. JOHN DRENNEN, ET AL. Crawford circuit court. Printed by Stillwell & Wassell, Little Rock, Ark. 23p. 8°.

Signed: Pike & Cummins, counsel for Drennen and others.

WALKER, JOHN W., AS COM'R OF 16TH SEC., APPELLANT VS. R. C. BYRD, J. ROBINS AND A. PIKE, SURV. APPELLEES. In the Supreme Court of Arkansas. No............, January term, 1854. Appeal from Pulaski circuit court. Printed by Stillwell & Wassell, Little Rock, Ark. 7p. 8°.

Signed: Pike & Cummins, counsel for appellees.

WALLACH, RICHARD L., AND OTHERS, APPELLANTS VS. JOHN VAN RISWICK, APPELLEE. Supreme Court of the United States. Term of 1874-5. No. 275. Brief for the appellants. Pike & Johnson, of counsel. Washington, D. C. Printed by W. H. Moore, 511 Eleventh street, 1874. 92p. 8°.

Cover title used.

WALLACH, RICHARD L., AND OTHERS, APPELLANTS VS. JOHN VAN RISWICK, APPELLEE. In the Supreme Court of the United States. Term of 1875-6. No. 62. Brief for the appellants, in reply. Albert Pike, Robt. W. Johnson, L. H. Pike, of counsel. [Washington, D. C.] Printed by W. H. Moore, 511 Eleventh street, 1875. 16p. 8°.

WEST, HECTOR R., ET AL., APPELL'TS VS. JOS. R. WILLIAMS, ET AL., APPELLEES, AND JOS. R. WILLIAMS, ET AL., APPELL'TS VS. HECTOR R. WEST, ET AL., APPELLEES. In the Supreme Court of Arkansas. No................, July term, 1853. Cross appeals from Pulaski circuit court, in chancery. Printed by Stillwell & Wassell, Little Rock, Ark. 24p. 8°.

Signed: Pike & Cummins.

WOODRUFF, WM. E. VS. WM. McD. PETTIT. In the Supreme Court of Arkansas. No................, July term, 1853. Error to Pulaski circuit court. Printed by Stillwell & Wassell, Little Rock, Ark. 6p. 8°.

Signed: Pike & Cummins, counsel for Pettit.

WORTHINGTON, E. vs. E. CURD & Co. In the Supreme Court of Arkansas. No................, January term, 1854. Appeal from Chicot circuit court. Printed by Stillwell & Wassell, [Little Rock, Ark.] 18p. 8°.

Signed: Pike & Cummins.

WYNN, WILLIAM vs. JOSIAH GARLAND. In the Supreme Court of Arkansas. No................, July term, 1852. Bill for title to the N. E. ¼ sec. 18. T. 16 S: R. 1 W. Printed by John M. Butler, Little Rock, Ark. 119p. 8°.

Signed: Albert Pike, solicitor for Wynn.

WYNN, WILLIAM vs. CHESLEY B. MORRIS, ET AL. In the Supreme Court of the United States. No................, December term, 1855. Error to the Supreme Court of Arkansas. Argument for William Wynn. John Wassell, printer, Little Rock, Ark. 90p. 8°.

Signed: Albert Pike, counsel for Wynn.

WYNN, WILLIAM vs. WM. F. MORRIS AND KEZIAH TAYLOR. In the Supreme Court of Arkansas. No................, July term, 1853. Printed by Stillwell & Wassell, Little Rock, Ark. 38p. 8°.

Signed: Albert Pike, counsel for Wynn.

MILITARY

ADDRESS. To the senators and representatives of the State of Arkansas in the congress of the Confederate States. 20p. 8°.

Signed: Albert Pike, Louisiana, 20th March, 1863.

Relates to charges and specifications preferred against Major General Thomas C. Hindman.

BATTLE OF PEA RIDGE, or Elkhorn Tavern, March 6, 1862. By Brig. Gen. Albert Pike. *In* La Bree. The Confederate soldier in the Civil War, p. 64-67.

CHARGES AND SPECIFICATIONS preferred August 23, 1862, by Brigadier General Albert Pike, against Major General Thomas C. Hindman. Richmond, Va. 1863. 13p. 8°.

LETTER TO THE PRESIDENT OF THE CONFEDERATE STATES. Fort McCulloch. Choctaw nation. July 3, 1862. 3p. 8°.

A circular letter signed: "Albert Pike," regarding Maj. Gen. Thos. C. Hindman.

MAXIMS OF MILITARY SCIENCE AND ART. *See* Manuscripts.

MUSTER ROLL OF CAPT. ALBERT PIKE'S COMPANY. *See* Manuscripts.

NEWSPAPERS.

THE ARKANSAS ADVOCATE. Little Rock, Arkansas.

Pike was Associate Editor in 1834, and Editor and owner from January 23, 1835 to April 20, 1837, or later.

THE MEMPHIS APPEAL. Memphis, Tennessee.

Pike was Editor-in-Chief about 1867-1868.

THE PATRIOT, Washington, D. C.

Pike was Associate Editor 1868-1870.

POLITICAL AND ECONOMIC.

ADDRESS BY THE PRESIDENT [ALBERT PIKE] OF THE STATE COUNCIL OF ARKANSAS, [AMERICAN PARTY], delivered at the first annual session, on the 30th April, 1855. Published by direction of the State Council. Little Rock, Ark., J. M. & J. D. Butler, printers, 1855. 15p. 8°.

ADDRESS ON THE SOUTHERN PACIFIC RAILROAD, delivered in the hall of the House of Representatives of the State of Louisiana. By Albert Pike. February 9, 1855. New Orleans, Emile La Sère, state printer, 1855. 21p. 8°.

DRAUGHT OF A DECLARATION OF INDEPENDENCE, proposed to the convention of the State of Arkansas, and withdrawn from its consideration. [By Albert Pike.] Little Rock, R. S. Yerkes & Co., printers, 1861. 13p. 8°.

THE EFFECT OF PARDONS AND AMNESTIES. [N. p., 186—?] 11p. 8°.

Signed: Albert Pike. Caption title used.

THE EMPHATIC REMONSTRANCE OF THE PEOPLE OF THE STATE OF ARKANSAS AGAINST INVASION OF THEIR RIGHT OF SELF-GOVERNMENT; addressed to the representatives of the other United States of America, in congress assembled. [By Albert Pike.] [N. p., about 1873?] 6p. 8°. Caption title.

INDICTMENT FOR TREASON . . . In the Circuit Court of the United States for the Eastern District of Arkansas. Albert Pike, defendant. [N. p., 1865.] 14p. 8°. Caption title.

Signed: Albert Pike.

KANSAS STATE RIGHTS. An appeal to the democracy of the south. By a Southern State-Rights Democrat [Albert Pike.] Washington, Henry Polkinhorn, printer, 1857. 39p. 8°.

ALBERT PIKE'S LETTER ADDRESSED TO MAJOR GEN. HOLMES. Little Rock, Arkansas, December 30, 1862. 1p. folio.

Printed on wall paper.

ALBERT PIKE'S LETTER ADDRESSED TO MAJOR GENERAL HOLMES. Little Rock, Arkansas, December 30, 1862. 7p. 8°.

SECOND LETTER TO LIEUT. GENERAL THEOPHILUS H. HOLMES. [Richmond, 1863.] 20p. 8°.

LETTER OF ALBERT PIKE TO THE CHOCTAW PEOPLE. Washington: Cunningham & McIntosh, 1872. 39p.

A LETTER TO THE PRESIDENT OF THE UNITED STATES. [By Albert Pike.] New York, C. S. Westcott & Co., printers, No. 79 John street, 1865. 19p. 8°.

LETTERS OF SAFEGUARD (issued to indian tribes west of Arkansas, August 12, 1861). *In* Moore, Frank. The Rebellion Record, v. 3, p. 400-401.

ALBERT PIKE

LETTERS TO THE PEOPLE OF THE NORTHERN STATES. [N. p., 1856.] 35p. 8°.
Signed: A. P. Caption title used.

LETTERS TO THE PEOPLE OF THE NORTHERN STATES. [N. p., 1856.] 48p. 8°.
Signed: A. P.

NATIONAL PLAN OF AN ATLANTIC AND PACIFIC RAILROAD, AND REMARKS OF ALBERT PIKE, MADE THEREON, at Memphis, November, 1849. Little Rock, Ark., Gazette and Democrat, print., [1849.] 16p. 8° Caption title.

ORDER No................ HEADQUARTERS, DEP'T INDIAN TERRITORY, Fort McCulloch, July 17, 1862. [2]p. wide 8°. Caption title and lines.
Signed: "By order of Brigadier-General Albert Pike, commanding department of Indian Territory:: G. A. Schwarzman, Major and Assistant Adjutant-General." A sarcastic "order," prompted by conditions in his Department.

OVERLAND ROUTE TO THE PACIFIC. [N. p., about 1857.] [1]+66p. 8°.
By a citizen of Arkansas: Albert Pike. Caption title used.

THE PAST TEACHING THE PRESENT AND THE FUTURE. *See* Manuscripts.

SOUTHERN AND WESTERN STATES COMMERCIAL CONVENTION, Charleston, South Carolina. Journal of proceedings during the week, commencing Monday, April 10th, 1854.
Addresses and resolutions by Albert Pike, p. 36-39, 64-70, 83, 84, 142-153, 157.

SOUTHERN AND WESTERN CONVENTION, Charleston, 1854. Resolutions of the Charleston convention upon the subject of the Southern Pacific Railroad, adopted April, 1854 [and] A bill to create and incorporate the Southern Pacific Railroad. 17p. 8°.
Presented to the Legislature of the State of Louisiana, Feb. 7, 1855, by Albert Pike.

SOUTHERN COMMERCIAL CONVENTION, New Orleans. Proceedings, January 8-15, 1855.
Addresses by Albert Pike, p. 5, 8-12, 16-20.

SOUTHERN COMMERCIAL CONVENTION, Savannah, Georgia, proceedings, December 8-12, 1856.
Debate by Albert Pike, p. 30-31, on slave trade, p. 39-40, on Southern Pacific Railroad.

STATE OR PROVINCE? BOND OR FREE? Addressed particularly to the people of Arkansas. By Albert Pike. [N. p.] 1861. 40p. 8°.

STATE OR PROVINCE? BOND OR FREE? APPENDIX. By Albert Pike. [N. p.] 1861. 21p. 8°.

THOUGHTS ON CERTAIN POLITICAL QUESTIONS. By a looker-on. [Albert Pike.] Washington, D. C. Geo. S. Gideon, printer, 1859. 104p. 8°.

TO THE AMERICAN PARTY SOUTH. Gideon, printer, 511 Ninth street, Washington, D. C. [1856.] 8p. 8°.
Signed: A. P.

B I B L I O G R A P H Y

TO THE PEOPLE OF ARKANSAS AND CALIFORNIA. [N. p., 1856.] 7p. 8°.
Signed: Albert Pike.

A TREATY OF FRIENDSHIP AND ALLIANCE, made and concluded at the North Fork village, on the North Fork of the Canadian river, in the Creek nation, west of Arkansas, on the 10th day of July, 1861, between the Confederates of America, by Albert Pike, Commissioner . . . and the Creek nation of indians . . . *In* Confederate States of America, Statutes at Large, Richmond, 1864, p. 289-310.

TREATY OF FRIENDSHIP AND ALLIANCE made and concluded at the North Fork village on the North Fork of the Canadian river, in the Creek nation, west of Arkansas, on the 12th day of July, A. D. 1861. By Albert Pike, Commissioner with plenary powers, of the Confederate States, and commissioners on the part of the Choctaw and Chickashaw nations. 25p. 8°.

Same in Confederate States of America, Statutes at large, Richmond, 1864, p. 311-331. Caption lines.

Same. Laws that united Choctaw and Chickashaw indians with the Confederacy. *In* Confederate Veteran, v. XI, no. 10, Nashville, Tenn., October, 1903, p. 449-458.

A TREATY OF FRIENDSHIP made and concluded at the Seminole Council House, in the Seminole nation, west of Arkansas, on the first day of August, 1861, between the Confederate States of America, by Albert Pike, Commissioner . . . and the Seminole nation of red men . . . *In* Confederate States of America, Statutes at large, Rich. 1864, p. 332-346.

TREATY WITH THE COMANCHES OF THE PRAIRIES AND STAKED PLAIN. Articles of a convention entered into and concluded at the Wichita agency, near the False Washita river, in the country leased from the Choctaws and Chickashaws, on the 12th day of August, 1861, between the Confederate States of America, by Albert Pike, their commissioner . . . and the Ne-co-ni, Ta-ne-i-we, Co-cho-tih-ca and Ya-pa-rih-ca bands of the Ne-un or Commanches of the Prairies and Staked Plain. . . . *In* Confederate States of America, Statutes at large, Rich. 1864, p. 354-362.

TREATY WITH THE COMMANCHES AND OTHER TRIBES AND BANDS. Articles of a convention entered into and concluded at the Wichita agency near the False Washita river, in the country leased from the Choctaws and Chickashaws, on the 12th day of August, 1861, between the Confederate States of America, by Albert Pike, their commissioner . . . and the Pen-e-tegh-ca band of the Ne-un, or Commanches, and the tribes and bands of Wichitas. . . . *In* Confederate States of America, Statutes at large, Rich. 1864, p. 347-353.

TREATY WITH THE OSAGES. Articles of a convention entered into and concluded at Park Hill, in the Cherokee nation, on the 2nd day of October, 1861, between the Confederate States of America, by Albert Pike, their commissioner . . . and the great Osage tribe of indians. . . . *In* Confederate States of America, Statutes at large, Rich, 1864, p. 363-373.

TREATY WITH THE QUAPAWS. Articles of a convention entered into and concluded at Park Hill, in the Cherokee nation, on the 4th day of October, 1861, between the Confederate States of America, by Albert Pike, their commissioner . . . and the Quapaw tribe of indians. *In* Confederate States of America Statutes at large, Rich. 1864, p. 386-393.

TREATY WITH THE SENECAS AND SENECAS AND SHAWNEES. Articles of a convention entered into and concluded at Park Hill, in the Cherokee nation, on the 4th of October, 1861 between the Confederate States of America, by Albert Pike, their commissioner . . . and the Seneca tribe of indians, formerly known as the Senecas of Sandusky, and the Shawnees of the tribe or confederacy of Senecas and Shawnees of Lewistown, or the mixed bands of Senecas and Shawnees. *In* Confederate States of America, Statutes at large, Rich. 1864, p. 374-385.

TREATY WITH THE CHEROKEES. October 7th, 1861. A treaty of friendship and alliance made and concluded at Tallequah, in the Cherokee nation . . . between the Confederate States of America, by Albert Pike, Commissioner with plenary powers, of the Confederate States. . . . 26p. 8°. Caption title.

Same in Confederate States of America, Statutes at large, Rich., 1864, p. 394-411.

THE TRUE MERITS OF THE CONTROVERSY IN ARKANSAS FOR THE CONSIDERATION OF HONEST MEN. By Pike & Johnson, attorneys and counsellors-at-law. Washington, 1874. 16p. 8°.

Contested election for the governorship of Arkansas, between Elisha Baxter and Joseph Brooks.

POETRY

(Collected)

No complete collection of Albert Pike's poems has been published up to this time. Dr. Susan B. Riley of Nashville, Tennessee, in 1934 compiled 247 typewritten pages of Pike verse from magazines, newspapers, manuscripts and miscellaneous sources, not found in his collected works. We are indebted to Dr. Riley for many of the additions to Mr. Boyden's listing. The imprint dates are more often very much later than when the verse was first written. One of the best known for example, *Hymns to the Gods,* did not appear in book form until 1872 but was actually written before 1831 when Pike was not yet 22 years of age. It was first published completely in a magazine of high literary standards, *Blackwood's Edinburgh Magazine,* Edinburgh, Scotland, in June of 1839, though at least two of the individual hymns had been published as early as 1830 in the *American Monthly Magazine.* The editor of *Blackwood's,* Professor Wilson ["Christopher North"] wrote of the *Hymns to the Gods* that "they entitle their author to take his place in the highest order of his country's poets."

PROSE SKETCHES AND POEMS, WRITTEN IN THE WESTERN COUNTRY. By Albert Pike. Boston, Light & Horton, 1834. 200p. 12°.

The dedication to Joseph M. Titcomb, of Newburyport, Mass., is very interesting in view of the many books and pamphlets Pike afterwards issued. He says: "My dear friend: as a token of ancient fellowship and friendship, I beg you to allow me to dedicate to you what will probably be my last (as it is my first) attempt at authorship, in the shape of a book." [In 1834 when Pike was 24 years of age.]

NUGAE. By Albert Pike. Printed for private distribution. Philadelphia, C. Sherman, printer, 1854. 363p. 12°.

A collection of his poems. Preface states that only 150 copies are published for private distribution, "and shall never consent that they be published in any other way."

HYMNS TO THE GODS AND OTHER POEMS. Albert Pike. Privately printed. [New York? 1872.] 98p. 8°.

Rubricated title page.

In a presentation note dated June 6, 1872 Pike wrote: "Please accept this copy of indifferent poems, printed for a few friends. . ."

HYMNS TO THE GODS AND OTHER POEMS. By Albert Pike. Privately Printed. Part I. [New York?] 1873. 98p. 8°.

HYMNS TO THE GODS AND OTHER POEMS. By Albert Pike. Privately Printed. Part II. [New York?] 1882. 254p. 8°.

Parts I and II are always bound together.

GEN. ALBERT PIKE'S POEMS. With introductory biographical sketch by Mrs. Lilian Pike Roome, daughter of the author. Illustrated. Little Rock, Ark., Fred W. Alsopp, publisher, 1900. 532p. 8°.

ALBERT PIKE

HYMNS TO THE GODS AND OTHER POEMS. By Gen. Albert Pike. Edited by Mrs. Lilian Pike Roome, daughter of the author. Illustrated. Little Rock, Arkansas, Fred W. Alsopp, 1916. 269p. 12°.

LYRICS AND LOVE SONGS. By General Albert Pike. Edited by Mrs. Lilian Pike Roome, daughter of the author. Illustrated. Little Rock, Arkansas, Fred W. Alsopp, 1916. 246p. 12°.

See Manuscripts.

(Individual)

ADDRESS TO TIME. *In* Bower of Taste, v. 3, No. 1, Jan. 9, 1830. p. 16.

[SONG:] "AFTER THE MIDNIGHT COMETH MORN." (For Senorita Carolina Cassard.) [By Albert Pike.] [Washington?] January, 1870. [2]p. 8°.

Another edition, differing only in typography.

Same in Hallum, John. Biographical and pictorial history of Arkansas, p. 223, Masonic Review, v. 65, no. 2, Mar., 1886, p. 90. New Age Magazine, v. 21, no. 1, July, 1914, p. 16. Saunders & Davis. Gems of genius, p. 583.

ALL WAIT. *In* National Freemason, v. 8, no. 5, Feb. 2, 1867, p. 67. 2 stanzas of 9 lines each. First line: "Truth dawns upon the human soul." Same as his "Truth." Not in any of his collected poems.

AMBITION. *In* American Monthly Magazine, v. 2, no. 5, August, 1830. p. 305.

Signed: "P." An article "Dreams," just preceding the poem is signed: "A," i. e. Albert Pike. 58 lines. First line: "There came a dark vision among the thick stars." Not in any of his collected poems.

ANNIE. *In his* Official Bulletins, v. 9, p. 177-178.

APOSTROPHE. *In* Graham's v. 20, No. 1, Jan., 1842, p. 12.

ARIEL. *In* Boston Pearl, v. 5, no. 7, Oct. 31, 1835, p. 52.

Same in Hallum, John. Biographical and pictorial history of Arkansas, p. 227.

AS THE SEASONS COME AND GO. [By Albert Pike.] [Washington?] September 6, 1875. [2]p. 8°.

Same in his Official Bulletins, v. 6, 451-452.

AULD LANG SYNE. [By Albert Pike.] As sung at Jas. C. McGuire's, January 8, 1869. [Washington? 1869.] [2]p. 8°.

Same in The Freemason (St. Louis), v. 5, no. 12, Dec. 1, 1871, p. 241. Library of Southern literature, v. 9, p. 4048-4049. Pike, Albert. Official Bulletins, v. 1, p. 544-545, and v. 6, 440-441. Texas Masonic Journal, Jan., 1885, p. 47.

AN AUNCIENTE FYTTE PLEASANTE AND FULL OF PASTYME OF A DOLLAR OR TWO. [By Albert Pike.] [Washington?] N. d. [3]p. 8°.

AUTUMN. *In* Boston Pearl, v. 5, no. 4, Oct. 10, 1835, p. 31.

Published in his collected poems as "Brown October."

AUTUMN. *In his* Official Bulletins, v. 7, p. 402-403.

THE BEAUTY OF LIBERTY. *In* Arkansas Advocate, Dec. 23, 1836.

BIBLIOGRAPHY

THE BRAVE MAN. *In* Voice of Masonry, v. 27, no. 11, Nov., 1889, p. 993.
4 lines only

THE BROTHERS. *In* American Monthly Magazine, v. 1, no. 11, Feb., 1830, p. 761-763.
Signed: "A. P." [Albert Pike.] 14 stanzas of 6 lines each. First line "Now night came down and the full moon beams." Not in any of his collected poems.

BUENA VISTA. *In his* Official Bulletins, v. 7, p. 517-519.
Also in Eggleston, Geo. C. American war ballads and lyrics, p. 151. Poetic and artistic masterpieces, p. 511. Rough and Ready Annual or Military Souvenir, p. 125.

CHANGES. *In* American Monthly Magazine, v. 2, no. 8, Nov., 1830, p. 548.
Signed: "P." March 6, 1830. 85 lines. First line: "Whence is the stream of years."

CHRISTMAS. By Albert Pike. [Washington? about 187—.] [2]p. 8°.
Written originally in 1849.
Same in his Official Bulletins, v. 7, 515-516. *Also in* Keystone, The, v. 20, no. 26. Dec. 25, 1886, p. 205; Light (Topeka, Kan.), v. 2, no. 24, Dec. 15, 1886, p. 281; Voice of Masonry, v. 25, no. 1, Jan., 1887, p. 54.

CLEOPATRE. [By Albert Pike.] [Washington?] September 3, 1875. [2]p. 8°.

A CONVERSATION IN THE FOREST. In The Knickerbocker, v. 33, no. 5, May, 1849, p. 382-388.
Published in his poems as "An evening conversation."

CRUISKEEN LAN. [By Albert Pike.] [Washington? about 1859.] [4]p. 8°.
Another edition. [By Albert Pike.] [Washington? about 1859.] [2] 8°.

THE DEAD CHILD. *In* Pope, W. F. Early days in Arkansas, p. 324.

DEATH IN THE DESERT. *In* Builder, The, v. 2, no. 5, May, 1916, p. 143.

A DIRGE. *In* Library of Southern literature, v. 9, p. 4057-4058.

DISSOLUTION OF THE UNION. *In* The Ladies' Companion, v. 12, Jan., 1840, p. 141.
13 stanzas of 8 lines each. First line: "Down with the stars and stripes from out the sky!" This line does not indicate the tenor of the poem which is admonitory. These lines preface the poem: "The following stanzas were written at the time when the Confederacy seemed on the verge of dissolution. Happily there is no call for such language now; yet the publication of the verses may not be without benefit."

DISUNION. *In* The Knickerbocker, v. 35, no. 3, Mar., 1850, p. 241.

DIXIE. *In* Brock, Sallie A. The Southern amaranth, p. 232.
Browne, F. F. Bugle echoes, p. 34.
Fagan, W. L. Southern war songs, p. 238.
Eggleston, George C. American war ballads and lyrics, p. 193.
Johnson, Helen W. Familiar songs, p. 580 (set to music).
Johnson, R. Campfire and battle field, p. 131.
Library of Southern Literature, v. 9, p. 4061.
Mason, Emily V. Southern poems of the war, varied eds.

Moore, Frank. Anecdotes, poetry and incidents of the war, North and South, p. 94.
Moore, Frank. Rebel rhymes and rhapsodies, p. 20.
Moore, Frank. The Rebellion record, v. 1, p. 106.
Moore, Frank. Songs and ballads of the Southern people, 1861-65, p. 38.
Simms, W. G. War poetry of the South, p. 92.
Wharton, H. M. War songs and poems of the Southern Confederacy, 1861-65, p. 29.

THE DREAM OF LIFE. *In* Arkansas Advocate, v. 6, No. 18, Aug. 7, 1835.

DREAM OF RUFUS. *In* Bower of Taste, v. 2, No. 16, Aug. 8, 1829, p. 491.

THE DYING EXPRESSION. In Boston Pearl, v. 4, no. 23, Feb. 14, 1835, p. 186.

Signed: "A. P." [Albert Pike.] 30 lines. First line: "Yes—death has set his fatal seal." Not in any of his collected poems.

EVERY YEAR. By Albert Pike. [Washington? about 1872.] [3]p. 8°.

EVERY YEAR. [By Albert Pike.] (A song old and new, the new in italic.) [Washington?] N. d. [2]p. 8°.

Of these two poems "Every year," the first has 7 stanzas of 8 lines each and the second, 8 stanzas of 8 lines each.

Same in Bromwell, J. H. Gems from the quarry, v. 2, p. 283. Hallum, John. Biographical and pictorial history of Arkansas, p. 225. James, J. G. Southern students handbook of selections for reading and oratory, p. 46-47. Library of Southern literature, v. 9, p. 4041-4043. One hundred choice selections, no. 17, p. 137. Perley, S. Poets of Essex county, Mass., p. 132-134. Pope, W. F. Early days in Arkansas, p. 321-323. Stedman & Hutchinson. Library of American Literature, v. 6, p. 489-490.

French and English text: La Chaine d'Union, v. 8, no. 11, Nov., 1879, p. 473. New Age Magazine, v. 21, no. 4, Oct., 1914, p. 156. Official Bulletins, by Pike, v. 4, p. 370-371. Voice of Masonry, v. 18, no. 5, May, 1880, p. 386.

Illustrated: Builder, The, v. 2, no. 1, June, 1916. Frontispiece. New Age Magazine, v. 2, no. 4, April, 1905, opp. p. 347. This poem is also found in nearly every masonic magazine published.

FANCIES ON FAME. *In* The Ladies' Companion, v. 14, Nov., 1840, p. 41-42.

Fifteen stanzas of 8 lines each. First line: "Once more upon the ocean!"

FANNY. *In* the Knickerbocker, v. 25, no. 5, May, 1845, p. 387.

FAREWELL TO NEW ENGLAND. *In* Duyckinck. Cyclopaedia of American Literature, v. 2, p. 521.

FATE OF THE PRESENT. *In* Voice of Masonry, v. 34, no. 6, June, 1896, p. 467.

Tribute to Theodore Parvin, 33°. 8 lines. First line: "The past is the fate of the present." Not in any of his collected poems.

"THE FINE ARKANSAS GENTLEMAN." [By Albert Pike.] [Washington?] N. d. [4]p. 8°.

Same in The Ashlar, v. 5, p. 476.

THE FREEMASON'S SON. *In* Mackey's National Freemason, v. 1, Dec., 1871, p. 126. The New Age Magazine, v. 13, no. 1, July, 1910, p. 76.

Five stanzas of 8 lines each. First line: "The monarch's son may revel in." Used in the reception of a louveteau in the Scottish Rite. Not in any of his collected poems.

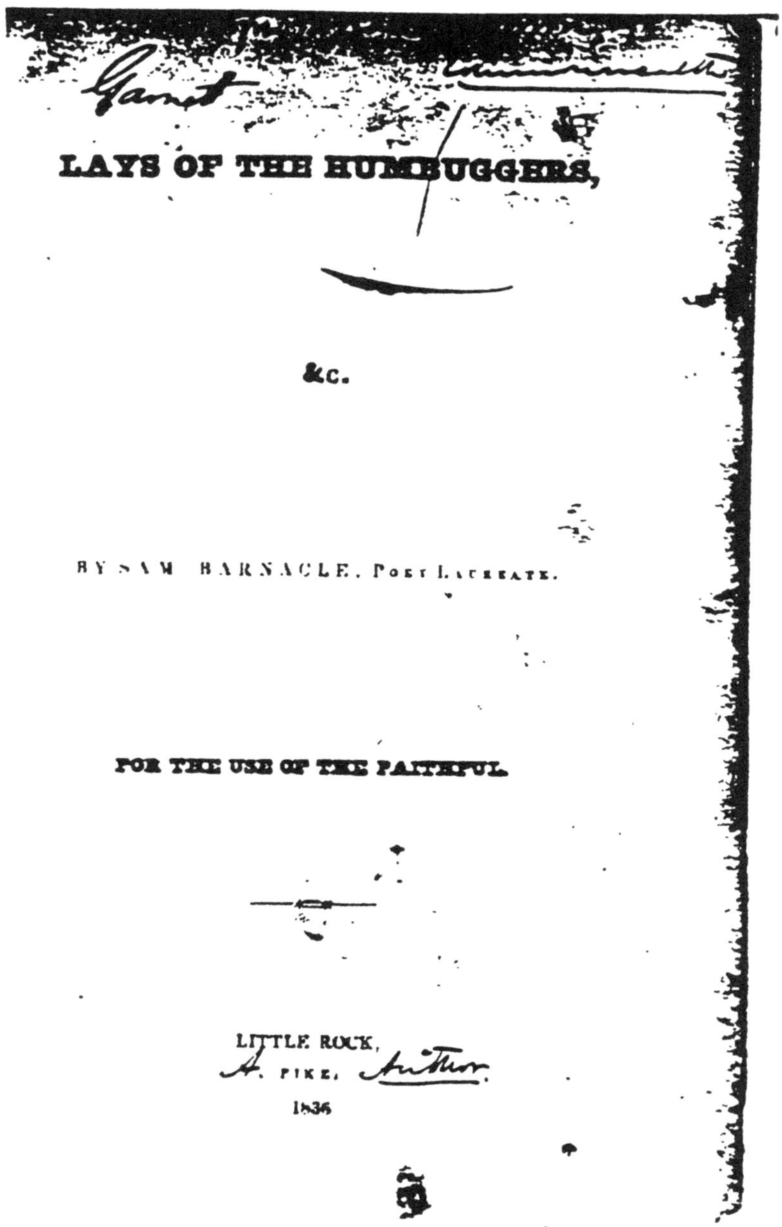

LAYS OF THE HUMBUGGERS,

&c.

BY SAM BARNACLE, Poet Laureate.

FOR THE USE OF THE FAITHFUL.

LITTLE ROCK,
PIKE,
1836

Courtesy of the Yale University Library

A SEPARATE PRINTING OF POLITICAL VERSE WHICH ORIGINALLY APPEARED IN THE ARKANSAS *Advocate,* 1836. ABOVE IS REPRODUCTION OF TITLE-PAGE FROM THE YALE UNIVERSITY LIBRARY'S COPY, WITH NOTATIONS IN PIKE'S HAND IDENTIFYING HIMSELF AS ITS AUTHOR. ONLY OTHER KNOWN COPY OF THIS SEPARATE PRINTING IS IN THE RARE BOOK COLLECTION OF THE LIBRARY OF CONGRESS.

"GOD COUNTS BY SOULS." *In* New Age Magazine, v. 21, no. 4, Oct., 1914, p. 165.
Three stanzas of 16 lines each. First line: "Who shall judge a man from nature." Same as "An unpublished poem by Albert Pike." Not in any of his collected poems.

A HOLY HOUSE TO BUILD. *In* Builder, The, v. 1, No. 10, Oct., 1915, p. 231; v. 4, no. 10, p. 285.
Freemasons' Repository, v. 2, No. 15, Nov. 15, 1872.
Illinois Freemason, v. 4, no. 5, Jan. 20, 1889.
Keystone, The, v. 31, no. 29, Jan. 14, 1888, p. 225.
Light (Topeka, Kan.), v. 5, no. 11, July 20, 1889, p. 85.
Mackey's National Freemason, v. 1, Oct., 1871, p. 32.
Masonic Jewel, v. 2, no. 8, Aug., 1872, p. 124.
Masonic Journal (Louisville, Ky.), v. 2, no. 3, Feb. 1, 1877, p. 45.
Masonic Journal (Portland, Me.), v. 2, no. 6, May, 1889, p. 167.
Masonic Review, v. 50, no. 4, May, 1877, p. 175.
Masonic Trowel, v. 1, no. 9, March, 1888.
New Age Magazine, v. 16, no. 1, Jan., 1912, opp. p. 57.
Pike, Albert. Official Bulletins, v. 2, pa. 2, p. 231-232 and v. 8, p. 380.
Square and Compass, v. 14, no. 9, Nov., 1905, p. 250.
Three stanzas of 9 lines each. First line: "We have a Holy House to build." Sometimes printed "The masons Holy House." Not in any of his collected poems. This poem is also found in nearly every other masonic magazine.

HYMN. *In* Boston Pearl, v. 5, no. 22, Feb. 13, 1836, p. 174.

HYMNS TO THE GODS. Bacchus. *In* American Monthly Magazine, v. 2, no. 8, Nov., 1830, p. 523.
Revised and published later in his series of "Hymns to the gods."

HYMNS TO THE GODS. Diana, Mercury. *In* American Monthly Magazine, v. 2, no. 7, Oct., 1830, p. 464.
Revised and published later in his series of "Hymns to the gods."

HYMNS TO THE GODS. *In* Blackwood's Edinburgh Magazine, v. 45, no. 284, June, 1839, p. 819-830; Griswold, R. W. Poets and poetry of America, p. 349-356. Knickerbocker, v. 35, nos. 4-6, April-June, 1850, p. 326, 443, 490.

AN INVITATION. *In* Knickerbocker, v. 25, no. 3, Mar., 1845, p. 202.

INVOCATION. *In* Knickerbocker, v. 25, no. 5, May, 1845, p. 432.

ISADORE. *In* Notes and Queries (Manchester, N. H.), v. 25, no. 6, June, 1907, p. 142.

JORDAN IS A HARD ROAD TO TRAVEL. [By Albert Pike.] Sung at Jonah Hoover's, Feb. 18, 1869. [Washington.] Cunningham & M'Intosh, printers. [2]p. 8°.

A LAMENT FOR DIXIE. [By Albert Pike.] [Washington?] August, 1877. [3]p. 8°.

LAYS OF THE HUMBUGGERS, &c. By Sam. Barnacle, [Albert Pike] Poet Laureate. For the use of the faithful. Little Rock, Pike, 1836. 8pp., 8vo.
First edition of the unrecorded separate publication. Not in Allen, Allsopp, Boyden or Sabin. Two known copies, one in the Library of Congress, the other in the Yale

University Library. The Library of Congress copy was originally in the collection of Dr. Joseph M. Toner, Washington physician. The Yale copy is of special interest because of the notation in Pike's handwriting, identifying himself as the author [see Illustration, page].

Six of the lays had appeared in six issues of the *Arkansas Advocate* in 1836. A seventh and unnumbered one was apparently composed for this separate printing.

Orlando Brown (1801-1867), original recipient of the Yale copy, according to the inscription on the title-page, was co-proprietor and editor of the Kentucky newspaper *Frankfort Commonwealth.*

LEGEND OF THE WILD HUNTER. *In* Boston Pearl, v. 5, Sep. 19, 1835, p. 3.

Published afterwards as "Legend of the wild rider," and as "The dead chase, a legend."

THE LIGHT OF DAYS LONG PAST. [By Albert Pike.] [Washington.] Cunningham & M'Intosh, printers [About 1866.] [1]p. 8°. *Same in* Light, The, (Topeka, Kan.) v. 2, no. 6, March 15, 1886, p. 68. *Same in his* Official Bulletins, v. 7, p. 480. Voice of Masonry, v. 29, no. 5, May, 1891, p. 360.

LINES. *In* Boston Pearl, v. 5, no. 6, Oct. 24, 1835, p. 42.

Seven stanzas of 7 lines each. First line: "The sea! the sea!"

LINES TO BOSTON. *In* The Ladies' Companion, v. 12, Dec., 1839, p. 87.

Fourteen stanzas of 8 lines each. First line: "Oh, Northern Athens, and Trimontane Gueen!" Not in any of his collected poems.

LINES WRITTEN ON THE ROCKY MOUNTAINS. *In* Griswold, R. W. Poets and poetry of America, p. 357.

LOVE. [Signed A. P.] *In* American Monthly Magazine, v. 2, no. 4, July, 1830, p. 266.

Sixty-eight lines. First line: "There came a train, on a pleasant eve." Not in any of his collected poems.

LOVE. *In* Boston Pearl, v. 5, no. 20, Jan. 30, 1836, p. 155.

LOVE RULES. *In* Bromwell, J. H. Gems from the quarry, v. 2, p. 21.

Four stanzas of 5 lines each. First line: "Evermore the people listen." Not in any of his collected poems.

Same in Voice of Masonry, v. 29, no. 2, Feb., 1891, p. 90.

THE MAGNOLIA. *In* Library of Southern literature, v. 9, p. 4054.

MA TRIESTE CHERIE. V........ [By Albert Pike.]. [Washington?] Feb. 26, 1869. [2]p. 8°.

THE MASON'S HOLY HOUSE. *See* A Holy House to build.

METRICAL (A) description of a fancy ball given at Washington, 9th April, 1858. Dedicated to Mrs. Senator Gwin. Franklin Philp, Washington, 1858. 40p. 4°.

Ascribed to Albert Pike.

MIDNIGHT, A LAMENT. *In* Boston Pearl, v. 5, no. 25, Mar. 5, 1836, p. 196.

MORNING, A LAMENT. *In* Boston Pearl, v. 5, no. 24, Feb. 27, 1836, p. 190.

B I B L I O G R A P H Y

MUSINGS. *In* Boston Pearl, v. no. 35, May 9, 1835, p. 281.

73 lines. First line: "We sit and watch the current of our life." Not in any of his collected poems.

NIGHT MUSINGS. *In* Boston Pearl, v. 4, no. 9, Nov. 8, 1834, p. 73.

143 lines. First line: "Ay, 'tis a glorious night." Not in any of his collected poems.

ODE. *In* Library of Southern literature, v. 9, p. 4058. New Age, v. 24, no. 6, June, 1916, p. 246.

First line: "When shall the nations all be free."

ODE. *In* American Quarterly Review of Freemasonry, v. 2, Oct., 1858, p. 161.

Two stanzas of 9 lines each. Used in the 19°, A. A. S. R.

ODE TO THE MOCKING BIRD. *In* The Essayist, v. 1, no. 7, July, 1832, p. 209.

ODES SUNG IN THE SUBLIME ORDER OF GOOD SAMARITANS. *In his* Official Bulletins, v. 3, p. 684-686.

"In part written, in part selected, and changed for Ill.·. Bro.·. Robert Macoy by Bro.·. Albert Pike."

THE OLD CANOE. *In* Masonic Age, v. 3, no. 1, Jan., 1881, p. 12. Masonic Journal, v. 2, no. 3, Feb. 1, 1877, p. 34. Masonic Review, v. 65, no. 2, Mar., 1886, p. 89. National Freemason, v. 9, no. 13, Sep. 28, 1867, p. 199. *His* Official Bulletins, v. 9, p. 371.

In this latter reference, Pike says: "Long before the war, the appended simple but charming verses appeared, it is said, without any signature or address, in the 'Arkansas Gazette,' at Little Rock. Their authorship continues to be ascribed to Albert Pike, although he has again and again in print disclaimed it. He is not their author."

ORA ATQUE LABORA. (Pray and work.) [and] Autumn. [By Albert Pike.] [Washington? about 187—.] [3]p. 8°.

First poem was originally written in 1844; the second one in 1842.

Same in Light, (Topeka, Kan. v. 1, no. 11, Oct., 1885, p. 86. The Knickerbocker, v. 26, no. 2, Aug., 1845, p. 138. Official Bulletins, v. 7, p. 401-402. Library of Southern Literature, v. 9, p. 4055-4056. Voice of Masonry, v. 26, no. 1, Jan., 1888, p. 64.

OUR AFTERNOON OF LIFE. *In* Masonic Journal, v. 2, no. 10, Sep., 1889, p. 294. Voice of Masonry, v. 28, no. 4, April, 1890, p. 317.

One stanza of 8 lines. First line: "Our afternoon of life has come."

POEM, read before the National Convention of Mexican War Veterans. [By Albert Pike.] January 16, 1874. [Washington?] [1874.] [3]p. 8°.

[POEM.] *In* Masonic Guide, v. 5, no. 3, Aug., 1894, p. 118. Masonic Review, v. 83, no. 5, June, 1895, p. 296. Square and Compass, v. 3, no. 3, May, 1894, p. 57.

Two stanzas of 13 lines each. First line: "The sky is blue, the stars are bright." Not in any of his collected poems.

POETS—PAST AND PRESENT. *In* Boston (The) Book, 1837. Edited by B. B. Thacher, p. 40-42.

Six stanzas of 6 lines each. Not in any of his collected poems.

ALBERT PIKE

THE PROGRESS OF POETRY. *In* American Monthly Magazine, v. 1, No. 9, December, 1829, p. 644-646 and v. 2, no. 9, Dec., 1830, p. 603-604.

Signed: A. P. 17 stanzas of 10 lines each. First line: "There shone a light on the eastern world." Not in any of his collected poems.

REUNION. [By Albert Pike.] Written to be sung at Charles W. Boteler's on Thursday evening, January 21, 1869. [Washington.] Cunningham & M'Intosh, printers, [1869] [1]p. folio broadside.

Seventeen stanzas of 7 lines each. Not in any of his collected poems in this form.

RE-UNION. [By Albert Pike.] Washington, January, 1869. [2]p. 8°.

Eight stanzas of 4 lines each. Same as certain of the stanzas in the preceding poem, with personal names and allusions omitted, as well as all the refrains in the former poem.

Same in his Official Bulletins, v. 6, p. 413.

ROBIN, THE. *In* The Essayist, v. 1, no. 12, Sep., 1833, p. 373.

Editor says: "From a collection of poems soon to be published." He refers to Pike's "Prose sketches and poems written in the Western country." Bost. 1834.

SEVENTY YEARS. *In* Voice of Masonry, v. 18, no. 8, Aug., 1880, p. 603.

Eight stanzas of 6 lines each. First line: "Seventy years to the very day." Not in any of his collected poems.

SHELLEY. *In* Library of Southern literature, v. 9, p. 4059.

SONG. *In* Boston Pearl, v. 5, Feb. 6, 1836, p. 163.

Published in his poems as "The husband to his wife."

SONG. [By Albert Pike.] [Washington?] N. d. [1]p. 8°.

Seven stanzas, with refrain to each stanza. First line: "Here's a health to the Prince of brave men and good fellows." Not in any of his collected poems.

SONG. *In* Boston Pearl, v. 5, no. 5, Oct. 17, 1835, p. 35.

First line: Let the dreaming astronomer number each star.

SONG. *In* Boston Pearl, v. 4, no. 2, Aug. 27, 1834, p. 19.

Two stanzas of 8 lines each. First line: "No, Mary, believe not I ever can change." Not in any of his collected poems.

SONG. *In* American Monthly Magazine, v. 1, new series, Feb., 1836, p. 146.

Two stanzas of 8 lines each. First line: "O'er the dark sea of life as man wanders in sorrow." Not in any of his collected poems.

SONG. *In* Hartford Pearl, v. 4, no. 1, Aug. 20, 1834, p. 7.

Three stanzas of 8 lines each. First line: "Oh, think not dear girl when the shadows of care." Not in any of his collected poems.

SONG. *In* American Monthly Magazine, v. 1, new series, Jan., 1836, p. 37.

Eight stanzas of 4 lines each. First line: "There is a wee and pretty maid." Not in any of his collected poems.

SONG. [By Albert Pike.] [Washington.] N. d. [1]p. 8°.

Same in his Official Bulletins, v. 7, p. 403.

First line: "When Autumn's chilly winds complain."

B I B L I O G R A P H Y

SONG [AND]. THE LIGHT OF DAYS LONG PAST. [By Albert Pike.] [Washington?] N. d. [2]p. 8°.

First line of first poem: "When Autumn's chill winds complain."

SONG. *In* Hartford Pearl, v. 4, no. 3, Sep. 3, 1834, p. 25.

Four stanzas of 6 lines each. First line: "Woman! woman!" Not in any of his collected poems.

SONG. "OH, JAMIE BREWED A BOWL O' PUNCH." [By Albert Pike.] [Washington? about 1860.] [2]p. 8°.

SONG. *In* The Life-wake of the fine Arkansas gentleman. [Pike] p. 25-31.

First line: "A gentleman from Arkansaw, not long ago 'tis said." Generally known as his "Spree at Johnny Coyle's."

SONNET. *In his* Official Bulletins, v. 7, p. 423.

SONNET TO BEAUTY. *In* The Essayist, v. 1, no. 25, Oct. 23, 1830, p. 99.

SONNET TO THE RAIN. *In* Boston Pearl, v. 4, no. 29, Mar. 28, 1835, p. 233.

Fourteen lines. First line: "Sweet rain! the concentrated breath of heaven." Not in any of his collected poems.

THE SOUTHERN ISLAND. *In* The Ladies' Companion, v. 13, May, 1840, p. 45.

Six stanzas of 8 lines each. First line: "There is an isle circled by Southern seas." Not in any of his collected poems.

SOUTHRONS HEAR YOUR COUNTRY CALL YOU. *See* Dixie.

This is the first line of his "Dixie."

SPIRIT OF POETRY. *In* The Essayist, v. 1, no. 2, Dec. 5, 1829, p. 7.

SPRING. *In* The Essayist, v. 1, no. 12, April 24, 1830, p. 46

SUMMER. *In* American Monthly Magazine, v. 2, no. 5, Aug., 1830, p. 341.

Signed: A. P. 72 lines. First line: "The summer is fair in the sun-lit air." Not in any of his collected poems.

SUNSET. *In* Boston Pearl, v. 4, no. 41, June 20, 1835, p. 330. *In his* Official Bulletins, v. 7, p. 422-423.

Published in his collected poems as "Sunset in Arkansas."

TIME'S ORATION. *In* The Ladies' Companion, v. 12, Apr., 1840, p. 265.

Fourteen stanzas of 8 lines each. First line: "Oh! I am but a poor and simple wight." Not in any of his collected poems.

"TO A FRIEND HE COULD NEVER SAY NO." (Sung at Cornelius Wendell's, February 11, 1869.) [Washington.] Cunningham & M'Intosh, printers [1869] [1]p. 8°.

Nine stanzas of four lines each. First line: "I have travelled the prairies all over." Not in any of his collected poems.

TO AMBITION. *In* Hartford Pearl, v. 4, no. 10, Nov. 15, 1834, p. 81. Not in any of his collected poems.

ALBERT PIKE

To Apollo. *In* American Monthly Magazine, v. 2, no. 5, Aug., 130, p. 311. Library of Southern Literature, v. 9, p. 4060.

Published afterwards as part of his "Hymns to the gods."

To Ceres. *In* Duyckinck. Cyclopedia of American Literature, v. 2, p. 520. The Essayist, v. 1, no. 4, April, 1832, p. 106. Linton, W. J. Poetry of America, p. 115.

Published afterwards as part of his "Hymns to the gods."

To E. P. *In* The Essayist, v. 1, no. 12, Sept. 1833, p. 363.

Signed: A. P. 20 lines. First line: "How sinks the sad and lonely heart." Not in any of his collected poems.

To Flora. *In* Ladies Magazine, v. 3, no. 8, Sept., 1830, p. 423.

To J. M. T. In The Essayist, v. 1, no. 11, Mar., 1833, p. 338.

Signed: Arkansas, December, 1832, A. P. 2 stanzas of 8 lines each. First line: "Though my faults and my follies have broken the ties." Not in any of his collected poems.

To my cap. *In* The Essayist, v. 2, no. 5, Jan. 1, 1831, p. 17.

To my wife. *In* The Knickerbocker, v. 26, no. 3, Sept., 1845, p. 202.

Five stanzas of 10 lines each. First line: "Our shallop long with tempest tried." Not in any of his collected poems.

To Neptune. *In* American Monthly Magazine, v. 2, no. 5, Aug., 1830, p. 298.

Signed: A. P. Revised and published later as part of his "Hymns to the gods."

To Poseidon. *In* Library of Southern Literature, v. 9, p. 4044.

Part of his "Hymns to the gods."

To a robin. *In* Library of Southern Literature, v. 9, p. 4052.

To Somnus. *In* The Essayist, v. 1, no. 6, June, 1832, p. 172.

Signed: A. P. Published afterwards as part of his "Hymns to the gods."

To Spring. *In* Griswold, R. W. Poets and poetry of America, p. 357. Harper's Family Library, no. CXI, p. 298. Linton, W. J. Poetry of America, p. 117. Masonic Mirror and Keystone, v. 8, no. 18, May 4, 1859, p. 205. New Age Magazine, v. 16, no. 5, May, 1912, p. 485. The Pearl and Literary Gazette, v. 3, no. 17, Mar. 29, 1834, p. 139. Pray, Isaac C. Prose and verse, p. 35.

To the first coming flowers of Spring. *In* American Monthly Magazine, new series, v. 1, Jan., 1836, p. 30.

Revised and later published as "The first wild flowers of Spring."

To the mocking bird. *In* Blackwoods Magazine, v. 47, no. 293, Mar., 1840, p. 354. Griswold, R. W. Poets and poetry of America, p. 356. James, J. G. Southern students' handbook of selections for reading and oratory, p. 205-207. Library of Southern Literature, v. 9, p. 4046. Pike, Albert. Official Bulletins, v. 7, p. 516-517. Stedman & Hutchinson. Library of American Literature, v. 6, p. 486-487.

BIBLIOGRAPHY

TO THE SOUTH WIND. *In* American Monthly Magazine, v. 2, no. 1, April, 1830, p. 39.

Signed: A. P. 6 stanzas of 10 lines each. First line: "Fair wind that comest from over the sea." Not in any of his collected poems.

TO VENUS. *In* American Monthly Magazine, v. 2, no. 6, Sept., 1830, p. 376.

Signed: A. P. Published later as part of his "Hymns to the gods."

TRUTH. *In* Bromwell, J. H. Gems from the quarry, v. 2, p. 277.

Same as his "All wait," which see. Not in any of his collected poems.

AN UNPUBLISHED POEM OF ALBERT PIKE. *In* New Age Magazine, v. 6, no. 3, Mar., 1907, p. 290.

Three stanzas of 16 lines each. First line: "Who shall judge a man from nature." Not in any of his collected poems. Same as "God counts by souls."

VOICE (THE) OF THE AGE. *In* Masonic Mirror and Keystone, v. 3, no. 8, Feb. 22, 1854, p. 57.

Five stanzas of 6 lines each. Not in any of his collected poems.

THE WAIF RETURNED. [By Albert Pike.] [Washington?] August 16, 1875. [1]p. 8°.

Same in his Official Bulletins, v. 8, p. 330.

THE WIDOW MOTHER WATCHING HER FIRST BORN. *In* Boston Pearl, v. 4, no. 44, July 11, 1835, p. 353.

101 lines. First line: "It was a silent midnight of young June." Not in any of his collected poems.

THE WIDOWED HEART. *In* Foote, H. S. Bench and bar of the South and Southwest, p. 189-181. Library of Southern literature, v. 9, p. 4050-4052. Stedman & Hutchinson. Library of American literature, v. 6, p. 487-489.

"WILT THOU ON THY SWEET BOSOM WEAR?" [By Albert Pike.] [Washington?] November 13, 1874. [1]p. 8°.

Same in his Official Bulletins, v. 8, p. 330.

WORDS OF SYMPATHY. FOR . . . AND HIS DEAD CHILD'S MOTHER. *In his* Official Bulletins, v. 6, p. 450-451.

Three stanzas of 7 lines each. First line: "The young leaf lives in spring its little hour." Not in any of his collected poems.

YES, CALL US REBELS. *In* Brock, Sallie A. The Southern amaranth, p. 294-295. *Same in* Mason, Emily V. Southern poems of the war. Moore, Frank. The Rebellion Record, v. 1, p. 66 (appx.).

Five stanzas of 8 lines each. First line: "Yes, call us rebels! 'tis the name." Not in any of his collected poems.

MISCELLANEOUS

An address delivered by Albert Pike, esq., to the young ladies of the Tulip Female Seminary, and cadets of the Arkansas Military Institute, at Tulip, on 4th June, 1852. Little Rock, Wm. E. Woodruff, printer, 1852. 31p. 8°.

Commentaries on the Kabbala. *See* Manuscripts.

Crayon sketches and journeyings, Nos. 1-3. *In* Boston Pearl, v. 4, nos. 9, 11, 18, Nov. 8 and 22, 1834 and Jan. 10, 1835, p. 69, 88, 143.

Cursory thoughts. *In* Brownell, J. H. Gems from the quarry, v. 2, p. 381.

Dreams. *In* American Monthly Magazine, v. 2, no. 5, p. 298.

Signed "A" and directly following it is a poem ("Ambition" signed "P," that is Albert Pike.

Emigravit. *In* Brownell, J. H. Gems from the quarry, v. 1, p. 354.

Great thoughts selected or written by Albert Pike. *In* Voice of Masonry, v. 28, no. 2, Feb., 1890, p. 83-88.

Indo-Aryan Deities and Worship as Contained in the Rig-Veda. [By] Albert Pike. 1872. Louisville, Ky., 1930. xii, 650 p. *See* Manuscripts.

Irano-Aryan Faith and Doctrine as Contained in the Zend-Avesta. [By] Albert Pike. 1874. Louisville, Ky., 1924. xvi, 726 p. *See* Manuscripts.

Irano-Aryan theosophy and doctrine as contained in the Zendavesta. *See* Manuscripts.

A journey to Xemes. *In* Boston Pearl, v. 5, no. 23, Feb. 20, 1836, p. 180.

Lectures of the Arya. [By] Albert Pike. 1873. Louisville, Ky., 1930. iii, 340 p. *See* Manuscripts.

Letters from Arkansas, no. 1. *In* New England Magazine, v. 9, Oct., 1835, p. 263.

Letters from Arkansas [no. 2]. *In* American Monthly Magazine, Jan., 1836, p. 25.

Life in Arkansas. *In* American Monthly Magazine, v. 1, new series, Feb. and Mar., 1836, p. 154, 295.

Life's journey. *In* Square and Compass, v. 14, no. 5, July, 1905, p. 121-122.

The loneliness of old age. *In* Brownell, J. H. Gems from the quarry, v. 1, p. 390.

B I B L I O G R A P H Y

MEXICO. Anniversary of the capture of the capital. The veterans celebrate the event. Grand excursion to Marshall Hall. Interesting literary exercises. An oration by General Albert Pike. . . . Reprinted from the Washington Chronicle, Sept. 15, [1875]. 8p. 8°.

Oration by Pike, p. 2-7.

MORAL INFLUENCES. *In* Brewer, D. J. and others. World's best orations, v. 10, p. 3945. [From an address before Louisiana Legislature.]

NARRATIVE OF A JOURNEY IN THE PRAIRIE. *In* Arkansas Historical Association Publications, v. 4, p. 66-139.

Originally published in his "Prose sketches and poems written in the Western country" and afterwards running as a serial in the Arkansas Advocate, in 1835.

OLD AGE AND DEATH. *In* James, J. G. Southern students handbook of selections for reading and oratory.

THE PHILOSOPHY OF BOWLING. *In* American Monthly Magazine, v. 2, no. 10, Jan., 1831, p. 687; The Boston Pearl, v. 4, no. 13, Dec. 6, 1834, p. 103.

THE PHILOSOPHY OF A CIGAR. *In* American Monthly Magazine, v. 2, no. 4, July, 1830, p. 254.

Signed: Newburyport, "P."

THE PHILOSOPHY OF WALKING. *In* American Monthly Magazine, v. 2, no. 5, Aug., 1830, p. 313; Boston Pearl, v. 4, no. 13, Dec. 6, 1834, p. 104.

PROSE SKETCHES AND POEMS, WRITTEN IN THE WESTERN COUNTRY. *See* Poetry.

REAL ATHEIM HOPELESS, SOULLESS, GODLESS. *In* Square and Compass, v. 15, no. XI, Jan., 1907, p. 288-291.

TRUE GREATNESS PERFECTED BY UNMERITED MISFORTUNE. *In* James, J. G. Southern students handbook of selections for reading and oratory.

THE WALKING GENTLEMAN. *In* The Knickerbocker, v. 25, no. 3, March, 1845, p. 209, and v. 27, nos. 2, 3, 5, Feb., Mar., May, 1846, p. 140, 230, 398.

Thoughts on various subjects. Not signed, but the index to the magazine gives Pike as the author.

WESTERN SUPERSTITIONS. *In* Boston Pearl, v. 5, Sept. 26, 1835, p. 14.

WESTERN TRAVELING. *In* Boston Pearl, v. 4, no. 6, Sept. 24, 1834, p. 48.

MANUSCRIPTS

These manuscripts are in Albert Pike's own fine hand, written with a quill pen. Except as noted, all are in the Library of the Supreme Council at Washington.

[ANCIENT ALPHABETS.] 65p. Oblong 8°.

Each page ruled with a border of red. Bound in full morocco.

ANCIENT FAITH AND WORSHIP OF THE ARYANS, AS EMBODIED IN THE VEDIC HYMNS. [By Albert Pike.] 1872-3. 2v. and supp. [v. 3] 2162p. Roy. 8°.

V. 1, 26+698 p. V. 2, 12+p. 699-1384. [V. 3] 10+742 p. Ornamental title pages to each volume, varying slightly in design and coloring. Several illustrations in v. 1 and 2 the title pages and illustrations being done in pen and ink by E. B. MacGrotty, 33°, Hon∴ of Washington. The pages of all the volumes are ruled with a border in colored inks, paged in black, with many underscores of words in colored inks, all by the same pen artist. Bound in full purple morocco, panelled backs. Paper of fine heavy quality, with gilt edges.

[AUTOBIOGRAPHY. BY ALBERT PIKE.] 86 typewritten pages on legal size paper.

From stenographic notes dictated by Pike, April 26, 1886, when he was in a reminiscent mood. Not the same as his printed "Autobiography," and much more extensive. Bound in full morocco.

COMMENTARIES ON THE KABBALA. [By] Albert Pike. Louisville, Ky., 1878. 235 written pages. Roy. 8°.

The title page is handsomely done in india ink with an artistic border, also in india ink and the MS. pages are all mounted on extra sheets. Bound in full morocco. Gilt edges; not paged.

ESSAYS. By Albert Pike. Washington, D. C., about 1880. 2166p. Roy. 8°.

Written on fine ruled paper, all pages bordered in colored inks, pages not numbered. Dedicated to Vinnie Ream Hoxie, the famous sculptress. No title pages. All volumes bound uniformly in full blue morocco, gilt edges. Lettered on back: "Essays. Pike," with the volume number and number of essays in each volume, each volume lettered on front cover: "Vinnie. Pegni d'affetto."

V. 1. 469 p. Contents: Dedication, introduction, essays, 1-6. No. 1, of content in life; 2, Of honoring the dead; 3, Of self-education; 4, Of men's opinions of women; 5, Of wrecks and waifs of poetry; 6, Of self-investing.

V. 2. 476 p. Essays 7-12. No. 7, Of habits and their slaves; 8, Of the death of love; 9, Of symbols decaying into idols; 10, Of indian nature and wrong; 11, Of my books and studies; 12, Of law and lawyers.

V. 3. 441 p. Essays 13-18. No. 13, Of rowing against the stream; 14, Of shattered idols; 15, Of coin and currency; 16, Of greatness; 17, Of poverty and its compensations; 18, Of the policy of forgiveness.

V. 4. 464 p. Essays 19-23. No. 19, Of some old dramatists; 20, Of pay and reward for public service; 21, Of forces; 22, Of values; 23, Of ability to say "NO."

V. 5. 316 p. Essays 24-29. No. 24, Of pleasant and sad remembrances; 25, Of sympathy; 26, Of chance and school-teaching; 27, Of godlessness and retribution; 28, Of leaves and their falling; 29, Jubilee of scoundrelism.

SECTION OF BOOKSHELF IN THE ALBERT PIKE ROOM CONTAINING BOUND ORIGINAL MANUSCRIPTS OF HIS TRANSLATIONS FROM THE ANCIENT HEBREW AND SANSKRIT, HIS COMMENTARIES ON THE KABALLAH, MAXIMS OF THE ROMAN LAW, ESSAYS, AND OTHER WRITINGS.

B I B L I O G R A P H Y

EXCERPTS. 176 written pages. Roy. 8°.

Selections in poetry and prose from famous writers, in various languages, epitaphs, etc., etc. One side of each page blank. Pages throughout ruled with a border of various colored inks, while many words are likewise underscored. Bound in ½ morocco, and lettered on back "Excerpts." Not paged.

EVERY YEAR. [See page 46.]

Apparently a final revision of the first, third, fourth, sixth and seventh stanzas each handwritten on separate sheet, each sheet signed and dated June 21, 1882. 5 sheets. In red cloth one-piece folding slipcase.

EXTRACTS FROM AND COMMENTS UPON THE KABBALA. Translated by Albert Pike. 1860. 383 written pages. Wide 8°.

All pages ruled with a border of red. Bound in full morocco. Not paged.

IRANO-ARYAN THEOSOPHY AND DOCTRINE AS CONTAINED IN THE ZEND AVESTA. [By] Albert Pike. 1874. 3v. 2344p. Roy. 8°.

V. 1, 32 + 757 p. insert of 4 p. at p. 634; v. 2, 8+p. 758-1514; v. 3, 10+p. 1515-2198+92 p. Ornamental title pages to each volume, varying somewhat in design and coloring, copy of a picture from Landseer's Sabaean Researches, and a map of "Imperium Persicum" in v. 1, and several illustrations in v. 3, the title page, illustrations and map, all being done in india ink by E. B. MacGrotty, 33°, Hon., of Washington, while the pages of all the volumes are ruled with a border in colored inks, paged in black, with many underscores of words in colored inks, all by the same pen artist. Bound in full purple morocco, with panelled backs. Paper of fine heavy quality, with gilt edges.

LECTURES OF THE ARYA. [By Albert Pike.] [About 1873.] 8v. 1499p. Wide 8°.

V. 1. Lecture I. The Aryan race. Its emigration and last division. The country character and manners of the Indo and Irano Aryans. 151 p.

V. 2. Lecture II. The Veda. The Aryan language. 166 p.

V. 3. Lecture III. The deities of the Veda, Agni-Indra. 152 p.

V. 4. Lecture IV. Vishnu, Vayu, Tvashtri, Rudra, Varuna, Mitra, Aryaman, the Acvins, Ushas, Pushan, and other deities. 163 p.

V. 5. Lecture V. The Vedic deities. Rudra: The Angirasas; the Acvinau; Soma, the Ribhus: Parjanya: Vata: Sarama: Sarasvati: the Apsarsas: Sinivali: Raka: Purusha: Prajapati: Hiranyagarbha. 177 p.

V. 6. Lecture VI. The Zenda-Avesta. The Gathas. The doctrine of Zarathustra. 159 p.

V. 7. Lecture VII. Ahura Mazda and the Amesha Cpentas. 165 p.

V. 8. Lecture VIII. The last four gathas and Legendary. 288 p. "Aryan notions of Philo Judaeus." 78 p.

Title page to each volume and much underscoring throughout, all probably done by E. B. MacGrotty, 33°, Hon., of Washington. Most of the sheets written on one side only. Bound in ½ blue morocco.

[LETTERS AND DOCUMENTS, PERSONAL AND OFFICIAL. By Albert Pike. From 1834-1891. Collected and arranged by R. Baker Harris, Librarian of the Supreme Council.]

The collection consists of as yet unnumbered pages, in excess of 5,000. Each separate letter is placed in an acetate transparent folder, and filed in Pendaflex suspended folders arranged chronologically by month and year, in steel cabinets. For the most part original letters, the collection includes also photostat copies of Pike letters located in other libraries and private collections. Additions are being regularly acquired by gift or purchase. The earliest letter is dated at Little Rock, August 18, 1834, and the latest dated

March 25, 1891 [Washington, D. C.] 8 days before his death. There is a card index to the names of recipients, and a subject index in progress. There is a separate group of undated and fragmentary items.

MAXIMS OF MILITARY SCIENCE AND ART. From the writings of Napoleon, Napier, Jomini, McDougall, Graham, Mitchell, Suchet, Bisset, Alison, and others, with occasional illustrations and applications. Compiled by Albert Pike. 1863. 6v. 2,182 written pages. Wide 8°.

In heavy cardboard covers, not bound.

MAXIMS OF THE ROMAN LAW AND SOME OF THE ANCIENT FRENCH LAW. As expounded and applied in doctrine and jurisprudence. Compiled by Albert Pike. [1876.] 13v. 3,340p. 8°.

In heavy cardboard covers, not bound. Preface states that he had been engaged on this work for many years. Not paged.

MUSTER ROLL of Capt. Albert Pike's company in the regiment of Arkansas volunteers . . . from the 31st day of August, 1846 . . . to the 31st day of October, 1846. 2p. folio.

Dated Monclavia, Mexico, October 31, 1846. In the National Archives at Washington.

MUSTER ROLL of Capt. Albert Pike's company in the Arkansas regiment of mounted volunteers . . . from the 31st day of October, 1846 . . . to the 31st day of December, 1846. 2p. folio.

Dated Hacienda de Patos, Mexico, December 31, 1846.
In the National Archives.

NOTES ON THE CIVIL CODE OF LOUISIANA. Made by Albert Pike in 1855, at New Orleans. 218 written pages 8°.

Title page and text throughout ruled with a border of red ink. Bound in ½ morocco.

THE PAST TEACHING THE PRESENT AND THE FUTURE. [By Albert Pike.] [About 1867.] 122p. 8°.

In heavy cardboard cover, unbound. The unpublished portions of his articles under that title which he wrote and published in the Memphis Appeal, Memphis, Tennessee while editor of that paper, shortly after the Civil War. Mounted on sheets in the same volume are the clippings of the published portions of the work. Political.

RULES AND ORDERS OF THE SUPREME COURT OF THE UNITED STATES. [N. p. about 1834?]

This printed copy of the Rules is interleaved with blank pages and additional blank pages at back, and paged in Pike's own hand, and contains 29 pages of MS. notes and amendments, by Pike.

THE SILVER WEDDING. A MASQUE. [By Albert Pike.] Acted April 8th, 1878.

Handwritten on 18 pages, one side of sheet only, 23 sheets in all. Bound in full morocco.

TO THE MOCKING BIRD. [Signed] Albert Pike, December, 1834. [4]p. Roy. 8°.

This poem is in 6 stanzas of 11 lines each. It is the earliest known specimen of Pike's handwriting. In blue cloth, one-piece folding slipcase.

B I B L I O G R A P H Y

TRANSLATIONS OF THE RIG-VEDA. THE MARUTS. [By] Albert Pike. [187—.] 4v. 2,641p. Roy. 8°.

V. 1. Hymns I. 6 to I. 100, p. 1-699.

V. 2. Hymns VI. 66 to X. 103. p. 700-1457.

V. 3. Hymns V. 52 to V. 87. p. 1-569.

V. 4. Hymns I. 142 to III. 54. p. 570-1184.

Ornamental title pages to each volume, varying slightly in design and coloring. All pages ruled with borders in colored inks. Title pages and rulings done by E. B. MacGrotty, 33°, Hon∴ of Washington. Bound in ½ red morocco. Paper of fine and heavy quality, mottled or marbled edges.

TRANSLATIONS FROM THE RIG-VEDA. FRIENDS OF INDRA: SVADHA: THE PURUSHA SUKTA: SAVITRI: NAMES OF RISHIS. [By] Albert Pike. [187—.] 562p. Roy. 8°.

Ornamental title page. All pages ruled with borders in different colors by E. B. MacGrotty, 33°, Hon∴ of Washington who also designed the title page. Bound in ½ red morocco. Paper of fine and heavy quality, mottled or marbled edges.

TRANSLATIONS OF THE RIG-VEDA. HYMNS TO TVASHTRI AND THE RIBHUS. [By] Albert Pike. [187—.] 716p. Roy. 8°.

Ornamental title page and all pages ruled with a border of colored inks, by E. B. MacGrotty, 33°, Hon∴ of Washington. Paper of fine and heavy quality, marbled edges.

TRANSLATIONS OF THE RIG-VEDA. OF THE DEVAS GENERALLY AND OF PASSAGES WHICH MENTION THE ARYA AND DASYU. [By Albert Pike.] [187—.] 632p. Roy. 8°.

Ornamental title page and all pages ruled with a border of different colors, by E. B. MacGrotty, 33°, Hon∴ of Washington. Bound in ½ red morocco. Paper of fine and heavy quality, marbled edges.

TRANSLATIONS OF THE RIG-VEDA. CONSECUTIVE. [By Albert Pike.] [1872-1886?] 7v. and 3 supp. v. 6,939p. Roy. 8°.

V. 1. Aryan light religions. Summary. Introductory chariots. Hymns I. 1 to I. 30. 786 p.

V. 1A. I. 1 to I. 30. Supplements. Agni: Apammapat: Vishnu: Vayu: The wives of the Vedas: Hiranya-Garbha and Praja-pati. 735 p.

V. 1B. Supplementary to Hymn I. 30. Varuna, Mitra and Aryaman. 492 p.

V. 1C. I. 1 to I. 30. Supplements. Dyava—Prithivi: Cyena: Ghrita: Hari: Yama: Cura and Sina: Vanaspati. 540 p.

V. 2. Supplements to I-30 continued. Vasishtha....................Foes of Indra. Hymns 31 to 33. Supplement to I-32 and 33. Indra. Hymns I-34, 35. 644 p.

V. 3. Hymns I-36 to I-52, inclusive. Supplement to I-40. Agni as Brahmanas-Pati and Brihas-Pati. 684 p.

V. 4. Hymns 53 to 77, inclusive. 659 p.

V. 5. Hymns 78 to 102, inclusive. 674 p.

V. 6. Hymns 103 to 120, inclusive. 724 p.

V. 7. [Hymns] I, 121 to I, 141, with I, 164, 1001 p.

Ornamental title pages, varying somewhat in style and coloring and all pages ruled with borders of various colored inks, the work of E. B. MacGrotty, 33°, Hon∴ of Washington. Bound in ½ red morocco. Paper of fine and heavy quality, marbled edges. A preface to vol. 7 states that he was engaged for more than fourteen years in the study of the Rig Veda and the compilation of works on this subject.

[VOCABULARIES OF INDIAN LANGUAGES. BY ALBERT PIKE.]. 119 written pages with two inserts of 28 and 6 pages respectively. Folio.

An autograph letter inserted begins: "These vocabularies were collected by me in 1857 and 1861, with great care and particularity and are correct."

[VOCABULARIES OF SANSCRIT WORDS. BY ALBERT PIKE.] 79 written pages on legal size writing paper.

In 7 parts, each part covered in brown paper and fastened with clips. Evidently made for his own use in translating the Rig Veda and other oriental writings.

A partial view of The Albert Pike Room in the House of the Temple. The room contains books, manuscripts, personal effects and other mementoes associated with his life and work.

BIBLIOGRAPHY

MASONIC

ADDRESSES AND REPORTS

ADDRESS. [By Albert Pike.] [N. p., about 1853.] 16p. 8°. Caption title.

An address on the subject of St. John's (Masonic) College, Batesville, Ark., and probably delivered there.

ADDRESSES, by Albert Pike, delivered before the Western Star Lodge, No. 2, of Ancient Free and Accepted Masons, June 24, 1851, and at the laying of the corner-stone of the Masonic and Odd Fellows Hall, May 20, 1852, in the city of Little Rock. Little Rock, W. E. Woodruff, printer, 1852. 23p. 8°. Cover title.

Same Extracts. In Masonic Mirror and Keystone, v. 3, nos. 31, 32, Aug. 2-9, 1854, p. 244, 252.

Same. Extract: Freemasonry, its danger, and the remedy. (From an address before Western Star Lodge, No. 2, Little Rock.) *In* Southern and Western Masonic Miscellany, v. 4, no. 5, May, 1853, p. 143-148.

ADDRESSES ON THE PRESENTATION OF A SWORD OF HONOR TO M. E. SIR BENJ. B. FRENCH, GRAND MASTER, on behalf of the Grand Encampment of Knights Templar of the United States, delivered before Washington Commandery of Knights Templar, No. 1, Wednesday, March 28, A. D. 1860, A. O. 742. Published by order of Washington Commandery, No. 1. Washington, Henry Polkinhorn, printer, 1860. 11p. 8°.

The presentation speech by Pike.
Same in Masonic Review, v. 23, no. 3, June, 1860, p. 165-169.

ARKANSAS GRAND LODGE. Proceedings 1853. Address to all affiliated freemasons in the State of Arkansas. Appx. p. 1-7.

Same in "Masonry in Arkansas," p. 94-103.

Report on Masonic law and usage, p. 58-61, 69-71.
Proceedings in 1854. Report of edicts, resolutions and decisions of the Grand Lodge, p. 1-15, at back.
Report on Foreign Correspondence, appx. p. 1-138.
Proceedings 1859. Address to the Grand Lodge, p. 48-50.

Same in Western Freemason, v. 4, no. 8, Feb., 1860, p. 253-254.

Proceedings 1860. Address to the Grand Lodge, p. 16-17. *Same in* Masonic Mirror and Keystone, v. 9, no. 48, Nov. 28, 1860, p. 575.

ARKANSAS GRAND CHAPTER. Proceedings 1853. Report on Foreign Correspondence, appx. p. 46-106. Report on Masonic law and usage, appx. p. 1-45. *Same in* Masonic Mirror and Keystone, v. 3, Nov. 4-17. [Reply of Albert Pike, to Bro. Mitchell's trictures in the "Signet" for April, 1854, on the report of the Committee on Masonic law and usage, in regard to the degrees of Royal and Select Master.] *In* Masonic Mirror and Keystone, v. 3, nos. 26-28.

Proceedings 1854. Address as Grand High Priest, p. 3-15. *Same in* Masonic Mirror and Keystone, v. 4, nos. 2-5, 1855.
Proceedings 1856. Report on Masonic law and usage, p. 27-33, 40-42.
Proceedings 1859. Report on Masonic law and usage, p. 38-47, 68-71.

A L B E R T   P I K E

AN EXAMINATION OF A REPORT OF A MASONIC COMMITTEE, made at Boston, in May, 1866. [By Albert Pike.] New York, Masonic Publishing and Manufacturing Company, 432 Broome street, 1866. 116+22+2p. 8°.

LAYING A CORNER-STONE (A.˙.& A.˙.S.˙.R.˙.) at the city of Washington, June 7, 1888. [Washington.] Joseph L. Pearson, printer, [1888.] 19p. 8°.

P. 4-13 contain an address by Pike.

Same in his Official Bulletins, v. 8, p. 371-379.

Same in Trestle Board, v. 2, no. 9, Sep., 1888, p. 257-261.

LECTURE [The evil consequences of schisms and disputes for power in masonry, and of jealousies and dissensions between masonic rites] of Bro.˙. Albert Pike, delivered by special request before the M. W. Grand Lodge of Louisiana, at its forty-sixth annual communication, held in New Orleans, February, 1858. Published by order of the Grand Lodge. New Orleans, printed at the Bulletin Book and Job Office, 1858. 68p. 8°.

Same in Louisiana Grand Lodge, proceedings, 1858, p. 69-135. Masonic Messenger (New Orleans), v. 1, no. 1, July, 1859, p. 2-27.

Same. What masonry is and its objects. Address originally delivered by Albert Pike at the Grand Lodge session of February 8, 1858. Re-delivered by M. W. Brother George A. Treadwell, Grand Master, February 4, 1919. New Orleans, A. W. Hyatt Stationery Mfg. Co., Ltd. 1919. 30p. 8°.

Does not contain the full text of the above "Lecture."

LECTURE IN THE HOLY ARCH DEGREE. *In* Masonic Mason and Keystone, v. 3, nos. 33-37, 1854. Southern and Western Masonic Miscellany, v. 5, nos. 1 and 2, July and August, 1854, p. 11-17, 38-45.

MASONIC VETERAN ASSOCIATION OF THE DISTRICT OF COLUMBIA. Transactions, 1879-87, [v. 1.] Address of the President, 1880, p. 20-23. Address of the President, 1881, p. 29-32. Introductory remarks of the President, 1882-83, p. 38-46. Address of the President 1883-84, p. 58-70. Address of the President, 1884-85, p. 78-86. Address of the President, 1885-86, p. 91-98. Address of the President, January 10, 1887, p. 114-129.

Transactions, 1887-1890, v. 2. Address, 9th January, 1888, p. 9-30.

Same. [Extracts.] Trestle Board, v. 3, no. XI, Nov., 1889, p. 321-330; v. 5, no. 10, Oct., 1891, p. 440-447; Voice of Masonry, v. 27, no. 10, Oct., 1889, p. 867-879.

Same in his Official Bulletins, v. 9, p. 321-337.

Same, printed separately: Address of the President [Albert Pike] of the Masonic Veteran Association of the District of Columbia, at the annual meeting, January 9, 1888. Washington, November, 1888. 26p. 8°.

Address of the President, January 14, 1889, p. 40-51.

Address of the President, January 13, 1890, p. 77-91.

Same, printed separately: Address of the President [Albert Pike] of the Masonic Veteran Association of the District of Columbia, at its annual meeting, January, 1890. Washington, Jos. L. Pearson, printer, 1890. 20p. 8°.

Addresses of the President [Albert Pike] of the Masonic Veteran Association of the District of Columbia, 1888, 1889, 1890. Washington, Gibson Bros., printers and bookbinders, 1890. 49p. 8° [Cover title.]

B I B L I O G R A P H Y

ORATION [Before the Grand Lodge of Odd Fellows of Arkansas,] August 8, 1850. [Little Rock, 1850.] 15+1p. 8°.
Caption title, "Oration."

ROYAL ORDER OF SCOTLAND, PROVINCIAL GRAND LODGE FOR THE UNITED STATES OF AMERICA. Records and minutes, 1879-1890.

Allocution of the Provincial Grand Master, 1879, p. 25-28; 1880, p. 42-44; 1881, p. 56-66; 1882, p. 80-84; 1883, p. 105-110; 1884, p. 141-146; 1886, p. 201-210, 214-220.

Same, printed separately: Allocution of the Provincial Grand Master [Albert Pike] for the United States of America. Ninth annual meeting of the Provincial Grand Lodge, Washington, D. C., October 18th, 1886. 21p. 8°.

1887, p. 239-248; 1888, p. 278-281, 294-296; 1889, p. 316-322. *Same in his* Official Bulletins, v. 10, 299-306.

1890, p. 366-387.

ST. JOHN'S DAY, Saturday, June 24th, 1871. Address in full of Dr. Albert G. Mackey, and condensed report of Gen. Albert Pike's address, delivered before the masonic fraternity of Sandusky, Ohio, and visiting brethren at Put-in-Bay, Ohio. 8p. 8°.

SUPREME COUNCIL FOR THE SOUTHERN JURISDICTION OF THE UNITED STATES. Transactions, 1860-1890.

Address of the Grand Commander [Albert Pike]:

1860 (original), p. 8-57.
(Reprint 1857-66) p. 84-119.

1861 (original 1861-66), Appx. A., p. 3-47.
(Reprint, 1857-66) p. 196-227, 231-242.

1865 (originals, 1861-66), Appx. B, p. 3-102.
(Reprint, 1857-66) p. 257-352.

1866 (originals, 1861-66), Appx. C, p. 1-35.
(Reprint, 1857-66), p. 405-438.

1868, p. 5-65.

Alloquiam of the grand Commander:

1870, Appx., p. 99-168.

Allocution of the Grand Commander:

1872, p. 6-39.

1874, Appx. A, p. 1-69.

1876, p. 4-42.

1878, p. 5-32.

Same in his Official Bulletins, v. 4, p. 3-30. *Same (extracts),* Masonic Record of Western India, v. 17, No. 5, Aug., 1880, p. 183-190.

1880, Appx. No. 1, p. 1-55.

Same in his Official Bulletins, v. 4, p. 395-416.

1882, Appx. A, p. 3-59.

Same, printed separately: Allocution of the Grand Commander [Albert Pike], Transactions of 1882. [Washington.] 62 p. 8°.

1884, Appx. No. 1, p. 3-74.

Same, printed separately: Allocution of the Grand Commander [Albert Pike], October 20, 1884. [Washington.] 74 p. 8°.

Same (extracts) in his Official bulletins, v. 7, p. 8-38; Masonic Review, v. 63, no. 2, Mar., 1885, p. 92-96; Texas Masonic Journal, v. 1, no. 1, Jan., 1886, p. 31-36.

1886, Appx. A, p. 3-54.

Same, printed separately: Allocution of the Grand Commander [Albert Pike], Session of 1886. [Washington.] 54 p. 8°.

Same in his Official Bulletins, v. 8, p. 1-54. [Extracts.] Texas Masonic Journal, v. 1. No. XI, Nov., 1886, p. 387-392.

1888, Appx. A, p. 1-40.

Same in his Official Bulletins, v. 9, Appx. p. 1-40.

1890, Appx., p. 1-54.

Same, printed separately: Allocution of the Grand Commander [Albert Pike] of the Supreme Council of the 33d degree of the Ancient and Accepted Scottish Rite of Freemasonry, for the Southern Jurisdiction of the United States, at its triennial session, October 20, 1890. Washington, Jos. L. Pearson, printer, 1890. 54 p. 8°.

Same [extracts]. Voice of Masonry, v. 29, No. 3, Mar., 1891, p. 212-217.

REPORT OF THE SOVEREIGN COMMANDER [ALBERT PIKE] ON THE DIFFICULTIES AT ST. JOSEPH, MISSOURI. *In* Supreme Council Southern Jurisdiction, Transactions 1870, p. 256-258.

THE TURNPIKE OF LIFE. *In* Mackey's National Freemason, v. 1, June, 1872, p. 452-453.

Being his response to a toast to which he was appointed to reply at the annual banquet of Lafayette Chapter, R. A. M., of the District of Columbia, December 19, 1872, the toast being to the life members of the Chapter and alluding to the turnpike of life.

WHAT FREEMASONRY WAS. Read at the meeting of the Masonic Veteran Association [of the District of Columbia] in February, 1887. [By Albert Pike.] *In* Transactions of the Association, p. 135-204.

WHAT OF THE NIGHT. The lesson of the Order of the Temple and of the Rose Croix. An address at a Lodge of Sorrow, in Louisville, Ky. *In* Voice of Masonry, v. 27, No. 6, June, 1889, p. 498-505.

OBITUARIES

(General)

ADDRESS. *In* Louisiana Grand Consistory, Ceremony of the Lodge of Sorrow, New Orleans, November 10, 1869, p. 4-8.

ADDRESS. At a Lodge of Sorrow. *In* Transactions of the Supreme Council, 1874, p. 84-89. Brownell, J. H., Gems from the quarry, v. 2, p. 166-168.

EULOGY. *In his* Official Bulletins, v. 4, p. 451-457. Transactions Supreme Council, 1880, p. 34-40.

HOMAGE TO THE ILLUSTRIOUS DEAD OF KENTUCKY, pronounced by Albert Pike, at the Lodge of Sorrow, held at Louisville, Kentucky, June 17, 1875. Washington, printed by W. H. Moore, 511 11th street, 1875. 14p. 8°.

Same in Masonic Newspaper [Extracts], v. 1, no. 37, June 14, 1879, p. 168-169; Masonic Eclectic, v. 1, no. 12, June, 1877, p. 553-559; Pike Albert. Official Bulletins, v. 3, p. 70-81.

TRIBUTE OF AFFECTION. *In* Masonic Jewel, v. 2, No. 6, June 15, 1872, p. 93-95. Transactions of the Supreme Council, 1872, p. 143-148.

A general tribute to the dead.

WORDS OF TRUTH SPOKEN OF THE DEAD. *In* Transactions of the Supreme Council, 1876, p. 86-94.

EX CORDE LOCUTIONES. Words from the heart spoken of his dead brethren, by the Grand Commander [Albert Pike] of the Supreme Council of the 33d degree for the Southern Jurisdiction of the United States. 1860 to 1891. [Press of J. J. Little & Co., New York, copyright, 1899.] Port. 8+358p. 8°.

Edited by Joseph C. Taylor, 33°, Hon.

The work in the main is a compilation of the separate obituary notices issued by Pike at various times, over his signature, either printed, stamped or autographed. The notices are prefaced in official form. The subjects of the obituaries appear only in the text of the notices. The following is a list of them arranged alphabetically:

(Individual)

AMES, ALFRED ELISHA, WILLIAM MARTIN PERKINS AND AUGUSTUS FREDERICK FITZGERALD. Washington, October 7, 1874. [3]p. Wide. 8°.

Same in his Official Bulletins, v. 2, pt. 3, p. 23-27.

BARBER, LUKE EDGAR. Washington, June 21, 1886. [3]p. Wide. 8°.

Same in his Official Bulletins, v. 8, p. 11-14. Texas Masonic Journal, v. 1, no. 8, Aug., 1886, p. 282-285.

BÉRARD, EUGÈNE-CHARLES. Washington, March 24, 1890. *In his* Official Bulletins, v. 10, p. 67-68.

BLACKIE, GEORGE STODART. Washington, June 23, 1881. [1]p. Wide. 8°.

Same in his Official Bulletins, v. 5, p. 5-6.

BRECKENRIDGE, JOHN C. *In* James, J. G. Southern student's handbook of selections for reading and oratory, p. 103-105. *From his:* "Homage to the dead of Kentucky."

BUIST, HENRY. Washington, June 10, 1887. [2]p. Wide. 8°.
Same in his Official Bulletins, v. 8, p. 19-23. Texas Masonic Journal, v. 2, no. 7, July, 1887, p. 229-233.

CAMPBELL, BENJAMIN RUSH. Washington, November 27, 1874. [2]p. Wide. 8°.
Same in his Official Bulletins, v. 2, part 3, p. 43-45.

CHRISTIE, JOHN. Washington, January 8, 1890. [2]p. Wide. 8°.
Same in his Occasional Bulletins, no. 10, p. 51-52. Official Bulletins, v. 9, p. 7-9. Ohio Council of Deliberation, Proceedings, 1891, p. 23-24.

CORSON, THOMAS J. Washington, January 8, 1880. [1]p. Wide. 8°.
Same in his Official Bulletins, v. 4, p. 57-58.

COTHRAN, WILLIAM AND WILLIAM GUSTAV EMILE TONN. Washington, February 7, 1881. [1]p. Wide. 8°.

DESAUSSURE, WILMOT GIBBES. Washington, February 4, 1886. [2]p. Wide. 8°
Same in his Official Bulletins, v. 7, p. 530-534.

ETTER, DANIEL FRANK. [Washington, 1890.] *In his* Official Bulletins, v. 10, p. 41-42.

FONDEY, TOWNSEND, AND ROBERT FARMER BOWER. Washington, June 19, 1882. [2]p. Wide. 8°.
Same in his Official Bulletins, v. 5, p. 365-366.

FRENCH, BENJAMIN BROWN. Washington, August 12, 1870. [1]p. 8°.
Same in his Official Bulletins, v. 1, p. 146-148.

FURMAN, CHARLES MANNING. Washington, July 10, 1872. [2]p. Wide. 8°.

GARFIELD, JAMES ABRAM. Notice of his serious illness from the assassin's bullet, which culminated in his death. Mimeographed. Washington, July 11, 1881. [2]p. Wide. 8°.

GIRARD, MICHEL ELOI. Washington, May 3, 1889. [2]p. Wide. 8°.
Same in his Official Bulletins, v. 9, p. 344-347.

GOULD, WILLIAM TRACY. Washington, December 15, 1882. *In his* Official Bulletins, v. 5, p. 431-432.

GRAHAM, ROBERT MCCROSKY. Washington, March 10, 1891. [2]p. Wide. 8°.

HARINGTON, THOMAS DOUGLAS. Charleston, January 14, 1882. [2]p. Wide. 8°.
Same in his Official Bulletins, v. 5, p. 13-14.

HARRIS, WILLIAM AUGUSTUS. [Washington, 1890?] *In his* Official Bulletins, v. 10, p. 36-38.

HIESTON, JACOB CASTLE. [Washington] January 16, 1884. *In his* Official Bulletins, v. 6, p. 44-445.

HILLYER, GILES MUMFORD. Washington. [May 21, 1871.] [1] p. Wide 8°.
Same in The Evergreen, v. 4, no. 7, July, 1871, p. 329-330. Pike. Official Bulletins, v. 1, p. 341-343.

HONOUR, JOHN HENRY. Charleston, November 27, 1885. [2] p. Wide. 8°.
Same in his Official Bulletins, v. 7, p. 525-527.

HORT, WILLIAM, ARTHUR BUSHE, GEORGE CHATTERTON, AND JOANNES G. PAPADAKIS. Washington, April 24, 1877. [3] p. Wide. 8°.

HUBBARD, HORACE HALSEY, AND ROBERT FARMER BOWER. Charleston [about 1882]. [2] p. Wide. 8°.
Same in his Official Bulletins, v. 5, p. 362-365.

IVES, EDWARD RUTLEDGE. Washington, 13th day of the Hebrew month (adar) A.·.M.·. 5630 [1870]. [2] p. 8°.
Same in Transactions of Supreme Council 1870, p. 227-228.

KEYSER, EDWARD S. Washington, March 14, 1881. [2] p. Wide 8°.

LAFFON, DE LADEBAT, CHARLES JOSEPH. Washington, January 20, 1883. [2] p. Wide 8°.
Same in his Official Bulletins, v. 5, p. 433-434.

LEWIS, JOHN LAWSON. Charleston, May 22, 1886. [2] p. Wide 8°.
Same in his Official Bulletins, v. 8, p. 9-11. Texas Masonic Journal, v. 1, no. 7, July, 1886, p. 241-243.

LEWIS, JOHN LIVY. Washington, June 17, 1889. [1] p. Wide 8.°
Same in his Official Bulletins, v. 9, p. 347-349.

McDANIEL, JOHN ROBIN. Washington, May 15, 1878. [3] p. Wide 8°.
Same in his Official Bulletins, v. 4, p. 42-43. Transactions Supreme Council, 1878, p. 69-72.

MACKEY, ALBERT GALLATIN. Washington, June 24, 1881, [2] p. Wide 8°.
Same in his Official Bulletins, v. 5, p. 6-8.

MACKEY, ALBERT GALLATIN. Washington, June 24, 1881. [1] Wide 8°.
Same in his Official Bulletins, v. 5, p. 57-58.

McMASTERS, STERLING Y. Washington, November 10, 1875. [3] p. 8°.
Same in his Official Bulletins, v. 3, p. 6-9.

MAUDE, JOHN BURTON. Washington, May 8, 1879. [2] p. Wide 8°.
Same in his Official Bulletins, v. 4, p. 50-52.

MELVILLE, JOHN WHYTE. Charleston, October 9, 1883. [2] p. Wide 8°.
Same in his Official Bulletins, v. 6, p. 6-8.

MILBITZ, ALLESSANDRO ISENSCHMID DE. Charleston, October 9, 1883. [2] p. Wide 8°.
Same in his Official Bulletins, v. 6, p. 4-6.

MILLIS, JAMES WESLEY. Washington, September 9, 1883. [3] 8°.
Same in his Official Bulletins, v. 7, p. 523-525.

MITCHELL, WILLIAM LETCHER. Charleston, November 1, 1882. [2] p. Wide 8°.
Same in his Official Bulletins, v. 5, p. 429-430.

MURRAY, JAMES CHARLES PLANTAGENET. Washington, August 9, 1874. [2] p. 8°.

NOYES, SAMUEL VERRILL. [Washington, February, 1886.] [By Albert Pike.] Cover title: "In Memoriam." 11 p. 8°.
Same in his Official Bulletins, v. 7, p. 573-577.

O'SULLIVAN, ANTHONY. Memphis, Tenn., 4th day of . . . A.˙.M.˙. 5626 [1866]. [1] p. Wide 8°.

PEARSON, JOSEPH LAWSON. [Washington, September 14, 1882.] [By Albert Pike.] 9 p. 8°. Cover title: "In Memoriam."
Same in his Official Bulletins, v. 5, p. 511-514.

PENN, JAMES. Washington, August 2, 1870. [1] p. 8°.
Same in his Official Bulletins, v. 1, p. 141-142.

PIERSON, AZARIAH T. C. Washington, November 27, 1889. [2] p. Wide 8°.
Same in his Occasional Bulletins, no. 10, p. 3-5.

POORE, BEN PERLEY. Washington, May 29, 1887. [3] p. Wide 8°.
Same in his Official Bulletins, v. 8, p. 15-18. Texas Masonic Journal, v. 2, no. 6, June, 1887, p. 196-199.

QUITMAN, JOHN ANTHONY. An address on the actions and character of John Anthony Quitman, Soverign Grand Inspector General, 33d degree. [By Albert Pike.] N. p. [1860.] 25 p. 8°.
Same in Transactions of Supreme Council (Original), 1860, p. 76-99.
Same in same (Reprint), 1857-66, p. 134-150.
Same. Extract from an address on. *In* American Freemasons Magazine, v. 6, no. 32, August, 1860, p. 79-84.
See also Manuscripts: Quitman, John Anthony.

RAMSAY, DAVID, JOHN SIEGLING, AND ACHILLE LEPRINCE. *In* Transactions of Supreme Council, 1868, Supplement, p. 21-26.

RICHARDSON, BENJAMIN BALL. Washington, February 17, 1880. [2] p. Wide 8°.
Same in his Official Bulletins, v. 4, p. 378-380.

RICHE, LÉOPOLD. Washington, D. C., March 20, 1885. *In his* Official Bulletins, v. 7, p. 142-143.

ROCKWELL, WILLIAM S. Washington, 22nd day of the Hebrew month Tebeth, A.˙.M.˙. 5630 [1870]. [3] p. 8°.
Same in Transactions of Supreme Council, 1870, p. 226-227.

ROOME, CHARLES. Washington, June 29, 1890. [2] p. Wide 8°.
Same in his Official Bulletins, v. 10, p. 548-551.

RUCHONNET, FRANCOIS LOUIS, FRANCIS ROBERT ST. CLAID ERSKINE, AND WILLIAM JAMES BURY MCLEOD MOORE. Washington, September 20, 1890. [2] p. Wide 8°.
Same in Herald of Masonry, v. 1, no. 3, Dec., 25, 1890, p. 25.

SAMORY, CLAUDE PIERRE. Washington, August 10, 1889. [2] p. Wide 8°.
Same in his Official Bulletins, v. 9, p. 349-352.

SCRUGGS, DANIEL EDWARD. Washington, November 9, 1871. [2] p. Wide 8°.
Same in his Official Bulletins, v. 1, p. 352-354.

SHAW, EBENEZER HAMILTON. Washington, February 21, 1876. [3] p. Wide 8°.
Same in his Official Bulletins, v. 3, p. 9-12.

SMITH, JONATHAN MOODY, AND ZEBULON MONTGOMERY PIKE. Washington, July 31, 1877. [3] p. Wide 8°.

SPOFFORD, RICHARD S. Washington, January 22, 1872. In his Official Bulletins, v. 1, p. 554-556.

TONN, GUSTAV EMILE. Washington, January 27, 1881. [2] p. Wide 8°.
Same in his Official Bulletins, v. 4, p. 699-700.

TOOMBS, ROBERT. Charleston, December 17, 1885. [2] p. Wide 8°.
Same in his Official Bulletins, v. 7, p. 527-530. Texas Masonic Journal, v. 1, no. 1, Jna., 1886, p. 7-10.

TUCKER, PHILIP C. *In* Mackey's National Freemason, v. 2, May, 1873, p. 397-403.

VAN HUMBEÉK, PIERRE. Washington, July 18, 1890. [2] p. Wide 8°.
Same in his Official Bulletins, v. 10, p. 558-560.

VIGNE, CHARLES JOHN, ANGEL MARTIN AND WILLIAM LEFFINGWELL. Washington, June 25, 1877. [2] p. Wide 8°.
Same in his Official Bulletins, v. 3, p. 362-364.

WATSON, HUGH PARKS, AND ANTHONY O'SULLIVAN. Memphis, Tenn., 4th day of . . . A.˙.M.˙. 5626 [1866]. *In* Transactions of Supreme Council, 1868, p. 62-63.

WHEAT, JOHN THOMAS. In memoriam. Washington, February 7, 1888. *In his* Official Bulletins, v. 8, p. 348-350.

WORSHAM, JOHN JENNINGS. Washington, 16 day of Ab. A.˙.M.˙. 5631 [1871]. [2] p. Wide 8°.
Same in his Official Bulletins, v. 1, p. 347-349.

OFFICIAL LETTERS AND NOTICES

1854, May 13, Little Rock, Ark. Letter to W. T. Gould, subject: Grand Chapters and the General Grand Chapter. *In* Southern and Western Masonic Miscellany, v. 5, no. 2, Aug., 1854, p. 48-49.

1859, December 27, Charleston, S. C. [2] p. folio. Address to the Supreme Councils of the world regarding representatives, uniformity of work and general fraternal intercourse.

1860, February 24, Washington, D. C. [1] p. Wide 8°. Notice to attend odjourned session of the Supreme Council, March 28, 1860.

1865, July 15, Charleston, S. C. [3] p. Wide 8°. Settlement of the dissentions in the two Supreme Councils of the Northern Jurisdiction of the United States.

1865, October 27, Charleston, S. C. [1] p. Wide 8°. Legitimacy of the Supreme Council for Cuba and the Antilles.

1866, January 8, Charleston, S. C. [3] p. Wide 8°. Notice of meeting of the Supreme Council, 1866.

1866, February 16, Charleston, S. C. 7 p. 8°. Legitimacy of the two contending Supreme Councils of the Northern Jurisdiction of the United States.

1866, March 4, Charleston, S. C. [1] p. folio. Appointing Richard H. Hartley, Special Representative near the Supreme Council of Peru, and authorizing him to confer the Scottish Rite degrees in Ecuador, Bolivia, and Chile.

1866, March 5, Charleston, S. C. [1] p. folio. Notice to several Supreme Councils of the appointment of Richard H. Hartley, as per preceding circular.

1866, March 12, Memphis, Tenn. [1] Wide 8°. Notice of meeting of the Supreme Council for the 3rd Monday in April, postponed from the 3rd Monday in February.

1867, September 1, Charleston, S. C. [1] p. folio. Invasion of rights of the Supreme Council, Southern Jurisdiction, U. S. A., by the Supreme Council of Belgium.

Same in Transactions of the Supreme Council, 1868, p. 205-208. Freemasons Monthly Magazine, v. 27, no. 1, Nov. 1, 1867, p. 9-11.

1867, [September 26] Memphis, Tenn. [1] p. Wide 8°. Qualifications necessary to receive the Scottish Rite degrees.

Same in Transactions of the Supreme Council, 1868, p. 189-190. Official Bulletins of the Supreme Council, v. 1, p. 91-92.

1867, [. . .] St. Louis, Mo. [1] p. Wide 8°. Conferring of degrees by bodies of the Northern Jurisdiction on candidates of the Southern Jurisdiction.

ALBERT PIKE

About 1884, wearing the official Decoration presented to him by King Kalakaua 33° of Hawaii, and a specially made insignia of the Triple Cross.

1867, [. . .] MEMPHIS, TENN. Controversy with George Frank Gouley. *In* Transactions, Supreme Council, 1868, p. 191-195; National Freemason v. 9, no. 18, November 2, 1867, p. 285.

1868, [ABOUT APRIL 2] MEMPHIS, TENN. [1] p. Wide 8°. Notice of Supreme Council meeting at Charleston, May 4, 1868.

1868, JUNE 30, CHARLESTON, S. C. [1] p. folio. Findings of the tribunal *in re* charges against George Frank Gouley.

1868, AUGUST 15, CHARLESTON, S. C. [1] p. folio. Notice of meeting of Supreme Council at St. Louis and Lodge of Sorrow to be held there.

1868, [. . .] [MEMPHIS, TENN?] [1] p. Wide 8°. Inspectors General and Deputies to make financial returns for degrees conferred.

1868, [. . .] MEMPHIS, TENN. [1] p. 8°. Asking for vote on the question of statutory delays between degrees.

1869, MARCH 1, CHARLESTON, S. C. 15 p. 8°. Letter of denunciation and appeal jointly by the Northern and Southern Supreme Councils against the Supreme Council for Louisiana, James Foulhouze and the Grand Orient of France. French and English text.

1869, MARCH 1 AND 8, CHARLESTON, S. C. AND BOSTON, MASS. Circular issued by Albert Pike and Josiah H. Drummond, Grand Commanders of the Northern and Southern Supreme Councils regarding the Grand Orient of France and the spurious Louisiana Supreme Council. French and English text. *In* Transactions Supreme Council 1868, p. 227-236; Transactions 1870, p. 181-180, 258-268, 280-284.

1869, APRIL 21, CHARLESTON, S. C. Revocation of the edict against the Supreme Council of Belgium. *In* Transactions of the Supreme Council, 1868, p. 219-220.

1869, APRIL 30, CHARLESTON, S. C. Legitimacy of the Supreme Council of Brazil, with *See* at Lavradio. *In* Transactions Supreme Council 1868, p. 220-222.

1870, [FEBRUARY 1], WASHINGTON, D. C. [2] p. Wide 8°. Conferring the degrees in too short a time and requiring the statutes to be observed in this connection.
Same in Transactions Supreme Council, 1870, p. 180-181.

1870, [MARCH . .], WASHINGTON, D. C. [2] p. Wide 8°. Notice of meeting of Supreme Council and of a Lodge of Sorrow to be held.
Same in Transactions Supreme Council, 1870, p. 168-170.

1870, [MAY? . . WASHINGTON, D. C.] [2] p. 8°. Requesting vote on statute regarding Court of Honour.

1870, MAY 2, CHARLESTON, S. C. 11 p. 8°. Letter of denunciation and appeal issued jointly by the Northern and Southern Supreme Councils against the Supreme Council of Louisiana, James Foulhouze and the Grand Orient of France.

1870, May 2, Charleston, S. C. 39 p. 8°. Letter of denunciation and appeal issued jointly by the Northern and Southern Supreme Councils against the Supreme Council for Louisiana, James Foulhouze and the Grand Orient of France, together with an appendix containing copies of letters, etc., of the Grand Orient of France, in French.

Same in his Official Bulletins, v. 1, p. 61-90.

1870, [June . .], Washington, D. C. [1] p. Wide 8°. Regarding returns or reports to the Supreme Council.

1870, July 14, Washington, D. C. [1] p. Wide 8°. Ritualistic matters.

1870, [July? . .], Washington, D. C. [1] p. Wide 8°. Regarding blank form to be appended to the ritual.

1870, December 19, Washington, D. C. [2] p. Wide 8°. Notifying that A. T. C. Pierson has no power to confer the degrees.

Same in The Evergreen, v. 4, no. 2, Feb., p. 90.

1871, January 1, Washington, D. C. [2] p. Wide 8°. Information for Inspectors and Deputies regarding conferring the Scottish Rite degrees.

Same in his Official Bulletins, v. 1, p. 155-157.

1871, January 5. Revoking his order of December 19, 1870, *in re* A. T. C. Pierson. *In* The Evergreen, v. 4, no. 3, March, 1871, p. 138.

1871, February 28, Washington, D. C. [1] p. 8°. Raising money for printing expenses.

1871, [About April 20], Washington, D. C. [1] p. 8°. Photograph cards of cipher.

1871 [June? . .] Washington, D. C. [2] p. 8°. Fees where there is a Grand Consistory.

Same in his Official Bulletins, v. 1, p. 355-356.

1871, October 25, Charleston, S. C. [3] p. Wide 8°. Regulations for the settlement of accounts.

Same in his Official Bulletins, v. 1, p. 363-364.

1871, November 10, Washington, D. C. [2] p. Wide 8°. Asking for aid for brethren of the Rite, sufferers from a calamity in Illinois, Michigan and Wisconsin.

Same in his Official Bulletins, v. 1, p. 364-365.

1872, March 10, Washington, D. C. [2] p. Wide 8°. Publication and expense of his "Book of the Words."

1872, March 11, Washington, D. C. [2] p. Wide 8°. Changing place of meeting of Supreme Council in 1872 from San Francisco to Louisville.

Same in his Official Bulletins, v. 1, p. 580-582.

1872, March 20, Washington, D. C. [1] p. 8°. Completion of his "Morals and Dogma," and their distribution.

B I B L I O G R A P H Y

1872, April 2, Washington, D. C. [1] p. Wide 8°. Nominations for the Court of Honour.

1872, June 15, Washington, D. C. [4] p. Wide 8°. Home for the Supreme Council.

Same in his Official Bulletins, v. 2, p. 17-18.

1872, November 28, Charleston, S. C. [2] p. Wide 8°. Disclaiming any conflict of the Scottish with the York Rite, etc.

The printed date is December 28, 1872, but was corrected to "November 28."
Same in Transactions of Supreme Council, 1874, appx. 73-75.

1872, December 16, Charleston, S. C. [2] p. Wide 8°. Conference of Supreme Councils proposed to be held in May, 1874.

Same in his Official Bulletins, v. 2, p. 10-11.

1872, December 28, *see* 1872, November 28.

1873, January 9, Washington, D. C. [1] p. Wide 8°. Asking for restoration to membership of George Frank Gouley.

Same in his Official Bulletins, v. 2, p. 17.

1873, February 28, Washington, D. C. 11 p. 8°. Letter to Josiah H. Drummond, regarding Andres Cassard, 33°. in connection with Scottish Rite matters.

1873, May 8, Washington, D. C. [2] p. Wide 8°. Stock in the Scottish Rite Sanctuary.

1873, June 17, Charleston, S. C. Regarding meeting of the Supreme Councils of the world. *In* Transactions of Supreme Council, 1874, appx. p. 75-76.

1874, January [. . .], Washington, D. C. Regarding Congress of Supreme Councils. *In* Transactions of Supreme Council, 1874, appx. p. 77.

1874, February 22, Washington, D. C. Regarding West Indies Supreme Councils. *In* Transactions of Supreme Council 1874, appx. p. 86-91.

1874, March 27, Washington, D. C. [2] p. Wide 8°. Notice of vote to change meeting of the Supreme Council to Washington in May, 1874.

1874 [June? . .], Washington, D. C. [1] p. 8°. Regarding publishing "Lecture on Masonic Symbolism."

1874, September 16, Washington, D. C. [2] p. Wide 8°. Embodying a communication from the Supreme Council of Belgium.

1874, October 9, Washington, D. C. [2] p. Wide 8°. Conferring of the Scottish Rite degrees by an Active Member or Deputy without observance of statutory delays, etc.

Same in his Official Bulletins, v. 2, p. 30-32.

1874, December 12, Washington, D. C. [1] p. Wide 8°. Forwarding copy of his "Lecture on Masonic symbolism," with data of cost of its printing, and reference to his Second Lecture.

1874, DECEMBER 15, WASHINGTON, D. C. 8 p. 8°. Submitting Articles of Confederation between Supreme Councils, to vote in recess.

1875, FEBRUARY 24, WASHINGTON, D. C. [2] p. Wide 8°. Submitting statutes and rules regarding finances of the Supreme Council.
Same in his Official Bulletins, v. 3, p. 14-17.

1875, APRIL 5, WASHINGTON, D. C. [1] p. 8°. Regarding publication of his Second lecture on Masonic symbolism.

1875, JULY 2, WASHINGTON, D. C. [2] p. Wide 8°. Establishment by the Supreme Council of France of a lodge in Honolulu, Hawaii, and the establishment by the Supreme Council, Southern Jurisdiction, of a Lodge of Perfection there and embodying copy of a letter from Supreme Council of France.
Same in his Official Bulletins, v. 3, p. 26-27.

1875, AUGUST 16, WASHINGTON, D. C. [4] p. Wide 8°. Same subject and embodying another letter from the Supreme Council of France.
Same in his Official Bulletins, v. 3, p. 30-35.

1875, NOVEMBER 8, WASHINGTON, D. C. [2] p. Wide 8°. Same subject.
Same in his Official Bulletins, v. 3, p. 35-37.

1875, NOVEMBER 19, WASHINGTON, D. C. [2] p. Wide 8°. Same subject, and the Articles of Alliance of Confederation of Supreme Councils.
Same in his Official Bulletins, v. 3, p. 38-40.

1875, NOVEMBER 20, WASHINGTON, D. C. Regarding publication of his Second lecture on masonic symbolism. *In* Masonic Chronicle, 1. 1, no. 9, January 1876, p. 144-145.

1876, FEBRUARY 2, WASHINGTON, D. C. [4] p. Wide 8°. Same subject of his controversy with Supreme Council of France, above noted.
Same in his Official Bulletins, v. 3, p. 46-52.

1876, MARCH 5, CHARLESTON, S. C. [3] p. Wide 8°. Forming another union of Supreme Councils from that of the Lausanne congress.

1876, MARCH 20, CHARLESTON, S. C. [2] p. Wide 8°. Same subject.
Same in his Official Bulletins, v. 3, p. 52-55.

1876, APRIL 18, WASHINGTON, D. C. [1] p. Wide 8°. Notice of meeting of the Supreme Council.

1876, MAY 13, WASHINGTON, D. C. [2] p. Wide 8°. Closing dispute with the Supreme Council of France.
Same in his Official Bulletins, v. 3, p. 55-56.

1877, JUNE 25, WASHINGTON, D. C. [2] p. Wide 8°. Proposing the creation of a Printing Fund.

1877, JUNE 25, WASHINGTON, D. C. [2] p. Wide 8°. Calling attention to certain portions of the law of the Supreme Council.
Same in his Official Bulletins, v. 3, p. 380-381.

[1877, ABOUT JUNE], WASHINGTON, D. C. [1] p. Wide 8°. List of books for sale by the Supreme Council, and note thereon.

1877, AUGUST 2, WASHINGTON, D. C. [4] p. Wide 8°. Supreme Council of Scotland and the League of Supreme Councils distinct from that at Lausanne, and embodying a letter from the Supreme Council of England and Wales.
Same in his Official Bulletins, v. 3, p. 445-449.

1877, OCTOBER 19, CHARLESTON, S. C. 19 p. 8°. Dei optimi maximi, universitatis rerum fontis ac originis ad gloriam majoref. [Signed: Albert Pike.] Or[ient] of Charleston, So. Carolina, October, 1877. [Printed at Washington, D. C.]
Text is in English. Relates to the action of the Grand Orient of France in its concessions to atheism.
Same in his Official Bulletins, v. 3, p. 514-529.

1878, JANUARY 1, WASHINGTON, D. C. [2] p. Wide 8°. Printing Fund.
Same in his Official Bulletins, v. 3, p. 382-384.

1878, MARCH 27, WASHINGTON, D. C. [1] p. Wide 8°. Notice of Meeting of the Supreme Council.

1878, MARCH 30, WASHINGTON, D. C. [2] p. 8°. Notice of organization of the Provincial Grand Lodge, Royal Order of Scotland.

1878, MAY 27, WASHINGTON, D. C. Recalling commission of Henry St. George Hopkins, etc.
In his Official Bulletins, v. 4, p. 49. Transactions of Supreme Council, 1878, p. 75.

1878, JUNE 12, WASHINGTON, D. C. [1] p. Wide 8°. Asking for photographs of all the Active members of the Supreme Council.

1878, JUNE 12. Early history of the Scottish Rite especially the Southern Jurisdiction. *In* Masonic Review, v. 51, no. 8, September, 1878, p. 352-357.

1878, JUNE 20, WASHINGTON, D. C. [2] p. Wide 8°. Appeal for aid for printing books.
Same in his Official Bulletins, v. 4, p. 58-60.

1878, JULY 22, WASHINGTON, D. C. [1] p. Wide 8°. Notice of election of J. C. Batchelor as Lieut. Grand Commander, etc.

1878, AUGUST 2, WASHINGTON, D. C. [2] p. Wide 8°. Supreme Council of Cuba and the creation of Supreme Councils in general.

1879, JANUARY 1, WASHINGTON, D. C. [1] p. Wide 8°. Simplification of titles.

1879, MARCH 15, CHARLESTON [WASHINGTON]. 21 p. 8°. "Titles of degrees, bodies and officers of the Ancient and Accepted Scottish Rite, to be used hereafter in the Southern Jurisdiction of the United States. Charleston [Washington.] 20 Adar, 5639 [1879]."

1880, JANUARY 3, WASHINGTON, D. C. [1] p. Wide 8°. Regarding issuance of diplomas of the 14°. Mimeographed.

1880, FEBRUARY 3, WASHINGTON, D. C. [1] p. Wide 8°. Regarding establishment of a Consistory at Minneapolis. Mimeographed.

1880, FEBRUARY 15, WASHINGTON, D. C. [1] p. 8°. Regarding the official Bulletin of the Supreme Council.

1880, MARCH 31, WASHINGTON, D. C. [2] p. 8°. Regarding the Cerneau Scottish Rite and embodying a letter from R. M. C. Graham of the Northern Supreme Council on the subject.

Same in his Official Bulletins, v. 4, 391-392.

1880, SEPTEMBER 1, CHARLESTON, S. C. [1] p. Wide 8°. Notice of meeting of the Supreme Council, 1880.

1880, NOVEMBER 15, WASHINGTON, D. C. [1] p. Wide 8°. Giving instructions and forms for filling in the proper data for use in compiling a Register of membership.

1881, MARCH 31, WASHINGTON, D. C. [1] p. Wide 8°. Asking for a vote on the restoration to membership of Henry H. Neal, 33°, Hon. Mimeographed.

1881, APRIL 27, WASHINGTON, D. C. [1] p. folio. Establishment in Florida of Cerneauism.

Same in his Official Bulletins, v. 5, p. 19-20.

1881, JUNE 25, WASHINGTON, D. C. [1] p. 8°. Appointment of Wm. M. Ireland as Secretary General of the Supreme Council.

Same in his Official Bulletins, v. 5, p. 26-27.

1881, AUGUST 16, CHARLESTON, S. C. [1] p. folio. Recognition of the Supreme Council of Tunis.

Same in his Official Bulletins, v. 5, p. 179-180.

1881, SEPTEMBER 1, [WASHINGTON, D. C.] 12 p. 8°. A letter from the Grand Commander [Albert Pike] of the Supreme Council, 33d for the Southern Jurisdiction, U. S. A. to the Grand Master of the Kadosh of Maryland.

Relates to difficulties in Scottish Rite masonry in Maryland.

1881, SEPTEMBER 6, CHARLESTON, S. C. [2] p. Wide 8°. Regarding the Grand Consistory of Maryland requiring candidates for the Rite to be Knights Templar.

1881, OCTOBER 15, WASHINGTON, D. C. [1] p. 8°. Regarding returns or reports to the Treasurer General of the Supreme Council.

Same in his Official Bulletins, v. 5, p. 374.

1882, JANUARY 3, WASHINGTON, D. C. [3] p. Wide 8°. Commending a plan for the establishment of the Garfield Masonic Memorial Institute, and embodying a letter from those proposing the plan.

1882, JANUARY 10, CHARLESTON, S. C. [1] p. Wide 8°. Regarding a home for the Supreme Council.

1882, MARCH 28, WASHINGTON, D. C. [1] p. Wide 8°. Same subject.

1882, June 30, Washington, D. C. [2] p. Wide 8°. Suspension of the bodies of the Rite in Augusta, Georgia.

1882, July 10, Washington, D. C. [1] p. Wide 8°. Regarding reports of Active members of the Supreme Council.
Same in his Official Bulletins, v. 5, p. 375-376.

1882, July 30, Washington, D. C. [1] p. Wide 8°. Legitimacy of the two contending bodies of the Rite in Spain.

1882, July 31, Washington, D. C. [2] p. Wide 8°. Transmitting a letter regarding Cerneauism in Canada.

1882, August 20, Washington, D. C. [2] p. Wide 8°. Regarding the Home or Building Fund of the Supreme Council.

1882, September 1, Charleston, S. C. [2] p. Wide 8°. Regarding the approaching session of the Supreme Council, 1882.

1883, February 25, Charleston, S. C. [1] p. folio. Recognition of the Supreme Council of Spain.
Same in his Official Bulletins, v. 5, p. 457-458.

1883, March 19, Washington, D. C. [2] p. Wide 8°. Purchase of a home or House of the Temple for the Supreme Council.
Same in his Official Bulletins, v. 5, p. 452-454.

1883, May 16, Washington, D. C. [1] p. Wide 8°. Presentation of a cabinet of minerals by Thomas H. Caswells.
Same in his Official Bulletins, v. 5, p. 487-488.

1883, June 4, Charleston, S. C. [2] p. Wide 8°. Expulsion of certain members for joining the Cerneau Scottish Rite.
Same in his Official Bulletins, v. 5, p. 488-490.

1883, October 31, Charleston, S. C. 13 p. 8°. Legitimacy of the Supreme Council of Cuba.
Same in his Official Bulletins, v. 6, p. 87-95.

1883, October 31, Charleston, S. C. [1] p. Wide 8°. Expulsion of Frederick Widdows for joining Cerneau Scottish Rite.
Same in his Official Bulletins, v. 6, p. 16-17.

1883, November 1, Charleston, S. C. [2] p. Wide 8°. Spurious Scottish Rite bodies.

1883, November 1, Charleston, S. C. [2] p. Wide 8°. Regarding the connections of certain named members in Washington, D. C., with the spurious Scottish Rite.
Same in his Official Bulletins, v. 6, p. 15-16.

1884, JANUARY 1, WASHINGTON, D. C. [1] p. Wide 8°. Issuance of certificates to the wives, daughters, etc., of Scottish Rite masons.
Same. [1] p. Wide 8°. Another edition varying slightly in the wording.
Same. [1] p. Wide 8°. Another edition varying slightly in the wording.
Same in his Official Bulletins, v. 6, p. 28-29.

1884, FEBRUARY 27, WASHINGTON, D. C. [3] p. Wide 8°. Regarding the Home or House of the Temple of the Supreme Council and the erection of a library building.
Same in his Official Bulletins, v. 6, p. 524-526.

1884, MAY 9, CHARLESTON, S. C. [2] p. Wide 8°. Regarding the Cerneau Scottish Rite.

1884, MAY 9, WASHINGTON, D. C. [3] p. Wide 8°. Regarding difficulties in Maryland, of the Scottish Rite.

1884, MAY 9, WASHINGTON, D. C. [2] p. Wide 8°. Regarding spurious Scottish Rite bodies and certain pamphlets issued by Pike thereon.

1884, JULY 1, WASHINGTON, D. C. [1] p. Wide 8°. Regarding Cerneau Scottish Rite Supreme Councils.

1884, JULY 1, WASHINGTON, D. C. [1] p. Wide 12°. A reissue of the preceding circulated through Oregon being countersigned by "R. P. Earhart, Inspector General, Oregon."

1884, JULY 1, WASHINGTON, D. C. [2] p. Wide 8°. Regarding the desertion of members named, from the Grand Consistory of Maryland to the Cerneau Scottish Rite.

1884, AUGUST 1, WASHINGTON, D. C. [2] p. Wide 8°. Regarding the approaching session of the Supreme Council, 1884, and information in connection with the same.

1884, AUGUST 15, WASHINGTON, D. C. [1] p. Wide 8°. Regarding the Cerneau Consistory at Baltimore and transmitting the names of its members.

1884, AUGUST 16, WASHINGTON, D. C. [2] p. folio. Extract from a letter of Bro.˙. Albert Pike, 33°, Grand Commander of the Supreme Council for the Southern Jurisdiction, to Bro.˙. . . . at Minneapolis, Minnesota.

1884, AUGUST 25, WASHINGTON, D. C. [2] p. Wide 8° Transmitting names of members of spurious Scottish Rite in California.

1884, AUGUST 25, [WASHINGTON, D. C.] 11 p. 8°. Extract from a letter of Bro.˙. Albert Pike, 33° . . . to Bro.˙. Henry M. Aiken, 32°, Deputy of the Sup[reme] Council for East Tennessee. [Washington] 1884.
Relates to the "Cerneau" controversy.

1884, OCTOBER 27, WASHINGTON, D. C. Letter to John H. Honour, Former Sov.˙. Grand Commander conveying regards and testimonial presented by the Supreme Council. *In his* Official Bulletins, v. 7, p. 99-100. Texas Freemason, February, 1885, p. 117.

1885, January 1, Washington, D. C. [2] p. Wide 8°. Regarding a fund of fraternal assistance.
Same in his Official Bulletins, v. 7, p. 116-119.

1885, January 5, Charleston, S. C. [2] p. Wide 8°. Regarding the Supreme Council of Colon (Cuba).
Same in his Official Bulletins, v. 7, p. 121-124.

1885, January 6, Washington, D. C. [1] p. Wide 8°. Regarding publication of a Register of Membership.
Same in his Official Bulletins, v. 7, p. 125-126.

1885, February 25, Washington, D. C. [1] p. Wide 8°. Requesting a vote on the question of establishing a Consistory in Maryland. Mimeographed.

1885, March 20, Washington, D. C. [1] p. Wide 8°. Regarding fund of fraternal assistance.

1885, September 9, Washington, D. C. [1] p. Wide 8°. Regarding letters lost or stolen in the mails.

1885, September 10, Charleston, S. C. [4] p. Wide 8°. Decision on the question of residence or domicile.

1885, September 15, Washington, D. C. [2] p. Wide 8°. Regarding the conferring of the degrees of the Scottish Rite in groups for the purpose of forming a new body.
Same in his Official Bulletins, v. 7, p. 546-548.

1885, September 26, Charleston, S. C. [1] p. folio. Scottish Rite masonry in Guatemala and the Supreme Council of Costa Rica.
Same in his Official Bulletins, v. 7, p. 549-550.

1885, September 28, Washington, D. C. [2] p. Wide 8°. Scottish Rite masonry in California and Edwin A. Sherman, claiming to be Special Deputy.

1885, October 20, Washington, D. C. [1] p. Wide 8°. Expulsion of Franklin P. Keesee from the Scottish Rite.
Same in his Occasional Bulletins, No. 10, p. 64-65. Official Bulletins, v. 7, p. 554-555.

1885, October 25, Washington, D. C. [4] p. folio. Answering attacks on him from Cerneau Scottish Rite sources.

1885, November 30, Washington, D. C. [2] p. Wide 8°. To the several Supreme Councils, regarding Edward W. Atwood and his spurious Supreme Council.
Same in Official Bulletins of Supreme Council, v. 7, p. 556-559.

1885, December 1, Washington, D. C. [1] p. Wide 8°. Regarding publication of Register of Membership.

1886, January 1, [Washington, D. C.] [1] p. 8°. Notice to Inspectors, Deputies and Bodies.

1886, FEBRUARY 8, WASHINGTON, D. C. [1] p. folio. Regarding moneys due Supreme Council from Bodies of the Rite.

Same in Official Bulletins of Supreme Council, v. 7, p. 559-560.

1886, FEBRUARY 18, WASHINGTON, D. C. [2] p. Wide 8°. Scottish Rite in Japan, embodying a petition from members in Yokohama for a Grand Consistory there.

1886, FEBRUARY 19, WASHINGTON, D. C. [2] p. Wide 8°. Regarding granting of a petition for a Consistory in Fargo, N. Dakota, with copy of the petition.

1886, FEBRUARY 20, WASHINGTON, D. C. [1] p. Wide 8°. To the Inspectors and Deputies of the Supreme Council regarding the non-receipt of supplies ordered by Bodies of their jurisdiction.

1886, FEBRUARY 25, WASHINGTON, D. C. [1] p. Wide 8°. Notice of Secretary General's resignation and the appointment of Frederick Webber as such.

1886, MARCH 9, WASHINGTON, D. C. [2] p. Wide 8°. Requesting answers to certain questions about rituals and other supplies.

1886, MAY 24, WASHINGTON, D. C. [2] p. Wide 8°. Letter to Juan M. Grau, Grand Commander of the Supreme Council of New Granada.

Same in Official Bulletins of Supreme Council, v. 8, p. 233-235.

1886, SEPTEMBER 1, WASHINGTON, D. C. [2] p. Wide 8°. Notice of the approaching session of the Supreme Council, 1886.

1886, SEPTEMBER 2, WASHINGTON, D. C. [1] p. Wide 8°. Requesting contributions for the sufferers from the earthquake at Charleston, S. C.

Same in his Official Bulletins, v. 8, p. 68-69.

1886, NOVEMBER 17, WASHINGTON, D. C. [4] p. Wide 8°. Regarding recognition of the Supreme Council of Dominican Republic.

Same in his Official Bulletins, v. 8, p. 142-147. *Same in same*, v. 10, p. 55-60.

1886, NOVEMBER 20, WASHINGTON, D. C. [2] p. Wide 8°. Appeal for Fund of Fraternal Assistance.

Same in his Official Bulletins, v. 8, p. 66-67.

1887, JUNE 12, WASHINGTON, D. C. [1] p. Wide 8°. Notice of appointment of officers in the Supreme Council.

1887, SEPTEMBER 15, WASHINGTON, D. C. [3] p. Wide 8°. Regarding his "Beauties of Cerneauism," and comments on spurious Scottish Rite masonry.

Same in his Occasional Bulletins, No. 9, p. 3-7. Official Bulletins, v. 8, p. 335-339.

1887, OCTOBER 1, WASHINGTON, D. C. [3] p. Wide 8°. Letter forwarding a communication, translated, from the Supreme Council of Belgium, regarding a conference of all Supreme Councils.

1888, MAY 1, WASHINGTON, D. C. [1] p. Wide 8°. Regarding conferring the degrees on subjects of the British Crown.

Same in his Official Bulletins, v. 8, p. 342-343.

1888, September 15, Washington, D. C. [1] p. Wide 8°. Notice of the meeting of the Supreme Council, 1888.
Same in his Official Bulletins, v. 9, p. 1-2.

1888, September 20, Washington, D. C. [1] p. Wide 8°. Appeal for yellow fever sufferers in Florida.
Same in his Official Bulletins, v. 9, p. 19-20.

1888, September 30, Washington, D. C. 9 p. 8°. Giving a list of the legitimate Supreme Councils and their officers.

1889, January 20, Washington, D. C.. [1] p. Wide 8°. Regarding the circulation of a pamphlet and the recognition of the Supreme Council of the Dominican Republic.
Same in his Official Bulletins, v. 9, p. 20-21.

1889, June 3, Washington, D. C. [1] p. Wide 8°. Appeal for sufferers of the Johnstown, Penna., flood.
Same in his Official Bulletins, v. 9, p. 360-361.

1889, June 20, Washington, D. C. [1] p. Wide 8°. Regarding the holding of a convention of the Masonic Veterans of the United States.

1889, August 20, Washington, D. C. [2] p. Wide 8°. Regarding Cerneauism.
Same in his Occasional Bulletins, No. 10, p. 7-10. Official Bulletins, v. 9, p. 361-363. *Same in same,* v. 10, p. 11-13.

1889, December 20, Washington, D. C. [2] p. Wide 8°. Regarding the Supreme Council of Spain.
Same in his Official Bulletins, v. 10, p. 134-136.

1890, June 21, Washington, D. C. [1] p. Wide 8°. Regarding the Official Register of the Supreme Council.

1890, September 25, Washington, D. C. [1] p. Wide 8°. Notice to active members of the approaching session of the Supreme Council, 1890.

1890, September 25, Washington, D. C. [1] p. Wide 8°. Notice to members of the approaching session of the Supreme Council.

1890, October 15, Washington, D. C. [1] p. Wide 8°. Requesting donations of indian arrow-heads for the Museum of the Supreme Council.
Same in his Occasional Bulletins, No. 11, p. 6.

CERNEAU CONTROVERSY

AN APOLOGY—SO-CALLED. [Washington, 1883.] 5 p. 8°. Caption title.
Signed: Albert Pike, 33d, Grand Commander.

BEAUTIES OF CERNEAUISM. No. 1. [By Albert Pike.] [Washington, 188—.] 4 p. 8°. Caption title.

BEAUTIES OF CERNEAUISM. No. 2. [By Albert Pike.] [Washington, about 1886.] 3 p. 8°. Caption title.

BEAUTIES OF CERNEAUISM. No. 3. [By Albert Pike.] [Washington, about 1887.] 15 p. 8°. Caption title.

BEAUTIES OF CERNEAUISM. No. 4. 7 p. 8°. Caption title.
Signed: Albert Pike, Washington, 23rd July, 1887.

BEAUTIES OF CERNEAUISM. No. 5. [Washington.] 50 p. 8°. Caption title.
Signed: Albert Pike, 33°, Grand Commander, August 1, 1887.

BEAUTIES OF CERNEAUISM. No. 5. Supplement. [Washington.] 6 p. 8°. Caption title.
Signed: Albert Pike, 33°, Grand Commander, September 15, 1887.

BEAUTIES OF CERNEAUISM. No. 5. Appendix: The record. [Washington, about 1887.] 14 p. 8°. Caption title.
Signed: Albert Pike, Grand Commander. These last three items are often bound together.

BEAUTIES OF CERNEAUISM. No. 6. [Washington.] 94 p. 8°. Caption title.
Signed: Albert Pike, Washington, August, 1887.

BEAUTIES OF CERNEAUISM. No. 6. Appendix. [Washington.] 5+15+1 p. 8°. Caption title.
Signed: Albert Pike, 33°, Grand Commander, September, 1887.

THE "CERNEAU SUPREME COUNCIL, SO-CALLED. A caution to Master Masons. Charleston, [Washington] 1881, 17 p. 8°.
Signed ‡ (that is, Albert Pike) April 10, 1881.

CERNEAUISM. Pertinent questions to be asked by its victims. [Washington, about 1887.] 15 p. 8°. Caption title.
Signed ‡ (that is Albert Pike).

CHASTISEMENT OF A BEARER OF FALSE WITNESS. Washington, August, 1889. With appendix. 24 p. +15+1 p. 8°.
Signed: Albert Pike, 33°∴ Grand Commander, Washington, August 20, 1889.

A FEW MORE CERNEAUISMS. [Washington, 1885.] 12 p. 8°. Caption title.
Signed: Albert Pike, 33°, Grand Commander.

BIBLIOGRAPHY

Foulhouzeism and Cerneauism scourged. Dissection of a manifesto. New York, press of J. J. Little & Co., 10 to 20 Astor Place, 1884. 116 p. 8°.
Signed: Albert Pike, 33d.·. Grand Commander, 1st November, 1883.

Foulhouzeism and Cerneauism scourged. Dissention of a manifesto. New York. press of J. J. Little & Co., 10 to 20 Astor Place, 1889. 116 p. 8°.
Signed: Albert Pike, 33d.·. Grand Commander, 1st November, 1883.

A fragrant nosegay of CCXXV flowers culled from the twin-parterres of Cerneauism. [By Albert Pike.] [Washington, 188—.] 47 p. 8°. Caption title.

Getting recognized rapidly. Cold comfort for dupes. 11 p. 8°.
Signed: Albert Pike, 33°, Grand Commander. Dated Washington, D. C., May 24, 1886.

A historical inquiry in regard to the Grand Constitutions of 1786, p. 125-211.
Preface signed: Albert Pike, 33°.·. Grand Commander, Washington, 1st February, 1883.
Originally published in 1872 as an introduction to the Latin Constitutions of 1786, and retaining the same pagination.

History vs. Cerneauism. [Washington, 1885.] 22 p. 8°. Caption title.
Signed: ‡ (that is, Albert Pike).

The ignobility of Cerneauism exposed. Charleston, [Washington] September, 1889. 36 p. 8°.
Signed: Albert Pike, 33°.·. Washington, September 12, 1889.

An inaccurate historian. [Washington,] [188—.] 8 p. 8°. Caption title.
Signed: ‡ Albert Pike, 33°.

Indictment and proof. 18 p. 8°.
Signed: Albert Pike, 33°, Grand Commander, Washington, August 10, 1889.
Same in Voice of Masonry, v. 27, no. 10, October, 1889, p. 922-934.

Latest Cerneauisms. [Washington, 188—.] 19 p. 8°. Caption title.
Signed: ‡ (that is, Albert Pike).

Masonic origines. [Washington, about 1885.] 16 p. 8°. Caption title.
Signed: ‡ (that is, Albert Pike).
Same in Texas Masonic Journal, v. 1, nos. 3-4, March and April, 1886, p. 79-82, 117-120.

Masonic origines. [Washington, about 1886.] 26 p. 8°. Caption title.
Signed: Albert Pike.

Masonic origines. By Albert Pike. Published by the Supreme Council of the 33d degree for the Southern Jurisdiction of the United States. Second edition. Washington, 1887. 24 p. 8°.

The modern Caliban. [Washington.] 9 p. 8°. Caption title.
Signed: ‡ (that is, Albert Pike) 1st February, 1886.

OF CERNEAUISM. A memoir on the part of the Supreme Council of the 33d degree for the Southern Jurisdiction of the United States. New York, press of J. J. Little & Co., 10 to 20 Astor Place, 1884, 79 p. 8°.

Signed: Albert Pike, 33°, Grand Commander [etc.], Washington, 1st January, 1884.

OF CERNEAUISM. Supplement. [By Albert Pike.] [N. p. N. d.] 47 p. 8°.

The above two pamphlets are usually bound together.

PERTINENT QUESTIONS FOR IMPOSTERS TO ANSWER: SUGGESTED TO THEIR DUPES. From letters of the Grand Commander [Albert Pike] of the Supreme Council of the 33d degree for the Southern Jurisdiction of the United States. 17 p. 8°. Caption title.

Dated at Washington, 1884.

PERTINENT QUESTIONS TO BE ASKED BY THE VICTIMS OF THE TWIN BASTARDS OF CERNEAUISM. 16 p. 8°. Caption title.

Signed: Albert Pike, 33°∴ Grand Commander of the Supreme Council for the Southern Jurisdiction of the United States, Washington, 15th November, 1887.

A SLIGHT CONTRIBUTION TO THE HISTORY OF CERNEAUISM. [Washington, about 1885.] 16 p. 8°. Caption title.

Signed: ‡ (that is, Albert Pike).

SQUIRMINGS. [By Albert Pike.] [Washington, about 1889.] 15 p. 8°. Caption title.

THE SUP[REME] COUNCIL FOR FRANCE AND ITS DEPENDENCIES. *In re* Joseph Cerneau. [With notes by Albert Pike.] Or[ient] of Washington, 1886. 72 p. 8°.

Another edition having after the imprint: "Distributed by the Supreme Council for the Northern Masonic Jurisdiction."

RITUALISTIC AND CEREMONIAL

We are indebted to Mr. Fred P. Farrar 33° for additional entries and notes in this listing of ritualistic and ceremonial writings. The notes for reprintings, revisions, and new editions have been provided where possible. Notes on those which remain in doubt or are questionable have been omitted. More recently, the Pike material has been reprinted, but with other explanatory matter not of Pike's authorship.

CEREMONIAL OF A LODGE OF SORROW. [By Albert Pike.] [N. p. N. d.] 18 p. 12°. Caption title.

CEREMONIAL OF A LODGE OF SORROW, [By Albert Pike] held in memory of a Sovereign Grand Inspector General, deceased, as used on the 30th of March, 1860, for Ill.·. Bro.·. John Anthony Quitman, 33d, by the Supreme Council for the Southern Jurisdiction of the United States. New York, Macoy & Sickels, 430 Brooms street, 1860. 15 p. 8°.

Same in Supreme Council Southern Jurisdiction, Transactions, 1860, p. 65-76.

CEREMONIAL OF MASONIC BAPTISM [By Albert Pike] IN THE ANCIENT AND ACCEPTED SCOTTISH RITE OF FREEMASONRY. Charleston and New York, Edmund Jones & Co., printers and stationers, No. 26 John street, 1865. 42 p. 8°.

CEREMONIES AT THE OBSEQUIES OF A KNIGHT KADOSH. [Washington? 1879.] 13 p. Wide 8°.

Signed: Albert Pike.
Same Officia suprema at the obsequies of a Knight Kadosh. Or[ient] of Charleston [Washington], 1887. 18 p. Wide 8°.

CEREMONIES OF EXTINGUISHING AND RELIGHTING THE LIGHTS. [By Albert Pike.] Alternative. To be used by any chapter at its option, if preferred by it to the ceremonies heretofore observed. [Washington? 1885?] 15 p. 8°.

Reprinted in 1925 as optional ceremony.
Use discontinued in 1933.

FUNERAL CEREMONY AND CEREMONY OF A LODGE OF SORROW OF THE ANCIENT AND ACCEPTED SCOTTISH RITE OF FREEMASONRY. [By Albert Pike.] Southern Jurisdiction of the United States of America. Charleston, S. C., 1868. 2 plates. 95 p. 8°.

FUNERAL CEREMONY OF THE ANCIENT AND ACCEPTED SCOTTISH RITE OF FREEMASONRY. [By Albert Pike.] Southern Jurisdiction of the United States of America. Honolulu [Hawaii]. H. L. Sheldon, printer, 1877. 38 p. 8°.

FUNERAL CEREMONY AND OFFICES OF A LODGE OF SORROW OF THE ANCIENT AND ACCEPTED SCOTTISH RITE OF FREEMASONRY. [By Albert Pike.] Southern Jurisdiction of the United States of America. Or[ient] of Charleston [New York or Washington.] 5646 [1886.] Illus. 83 p. 8°.

Reprinted 1947.

ALBERT PIKE

LATTER DAY RITUALS. In Brownell, J. H. Gems from the quarry, v. 2, p. 467.

LITURGY OF THE ANCIENT AND ACCEPTED SCOTTISH RITE OF FREEMASONRY, for the Southern Jurisdiction of the United States. [By Albert Pike.] Part I. I-III. Charleston, [New York, J. J. Little & Co., printers, 10 to 20 Astor Place.] A.˙. M.˙. 5638 [1878.] 223 p. 8°.

Rubicated title page. Colored plates and illustrations.

LITURGY OF THE ANCIENT AND ACCEPTED SCOTTISH RITE OF FREEMASONRY, for the Southern Jurisdiction of the United States. [By Albert Pike.] Part II. IV to XIV. Charleston [New York, Masonic Publishing and Manufacturing Co.] A.˙. M.˙. 5627, [1867.] 240 p. 8°.

Rubricated title page. Colored plates and illustrations.

LITURGY OF THE ANCIENT AND ACCEPTED SCOTTISH RITE OF FREEMASONRY, for the Southern Jurisdiction of the United States. [By Albert Pike.] Part II. IV to XIV. Charleston, A.˙. M.˙. 5638 [1878.] New York, press of J. J. Little & Co. 243 p. 8°.

Rubricated title page. Colored plates and illustrations. Copyright, 1877.

LITURGY OF THE ANCIENT AND ACCEPTED SCOTTISH RITE OF FREEMASONRY, for the Southern Jurisdiction of the United States. [By Albert Pike.] Part II. IV to XIV. Charleston A.˙. M.˙. 5638 [1878.] New York, press of J. J. Little & Co., 10 to 20 Astor Place. 243 p. 8°.

Rubricated title page. Colored plates and illustrations. Copyright, 1877.

LITURGY OF THE ANCIENT AND ACCEPTED SCOTTISH RITE OF FREEMASONRY, for the Southern Jurisdiction of the United States. [By Albert Pike.] Part II. IV to XIV. Charleston, A.˙. M.˙. 5638, [1878.] New York, Robert Macoy, 4 Barclay street. 243 p. 8°.

Rubricated title page. Colored plates and illustrations. Copyright, 1877. Copyright page says: "New York, J. J. Little & Co., printers, 10 to 20 Astor place."

Reprinted without color plates. Copyright page says "L. H. Jenkins, Inc., Printers and Binders, Richmond, Va. 21-1"

Reprinted without color plates, 213 p. [Appendix, 215/243 omitted] 1947.

LITURGY OF THE ANCIENT AND ACCEPTED SCOTTISH RITE OF FREEMASONRY, for the Southern Jurisdiction of the United States. [By Albert Pike.] Part III. XV to XVIII. Charleston, A.˙. M.˙., [1878.] New York, Robert Macoy, 4 Barclay street. 187 p. 8°.

Rubricated title page. Colored plates and illustrations. Copyright, 1877. Copyright page says: "New York, J. J. Little & Co., printers, 10 to 20 Astor place."

Reprinted without color plates. N.D. *Transactions* [Supreme Council] 1905, 123: Plates last used December 1904; 1927, 145: New edition in preparation, with revisions; 1937, 151: New edition.

Reprinted, without color plates. 1936. 190 p. Copyright page says: "W. F. Roberts, Inc., Washington, D. C."

Reprinted, 1956, with color plates. [Baltimore, Publication Press].

BIBLIOGRAPHY

LITURGY OF THE ANCIENT AND ACCEPTED SCOTTISH RITE OF FREEMASONRY, for the Southern Jurisdiction of the United States. [By Albert Pike.] Part IV. XIX to XXX. Charleston, [New York, J. J. Little & Co., printers, 10 to 20 Astor Place.] A.·. M.·. 5638, [1878.] 291+2 p. 8°.

Rubricated title page. Colored plates and illustrations.

Reprinted without color plates. N.d. *Transactions*, 1905, 123: Plates last used April 1902.

Reprinted, 1944, without color plates.

[THE MAGNUM OPUS. By Albert Pike.] [Philadelphia, 1857.] [604 p.] 4°.

No title page. The work is known as the "Magnum Opus," or great work. Only 100 copies printed. Each degree, from the 4th to the 32nd inclusive is paged separately. First Pike version of the esoteric work and lectures of the rituals of the Scottish Rite.

MORALS AND DOGMA OF THE ANCIENT AND ACCEPTED SCOTTISH RITE OF FREEMASONRY. Prepared [By Albert Pike] for the Supreme Council of the Thirty-Third Degree, for the Southern Jurisdiction of the United States, and published by its authority. Charleston, [New York, Masonic Publishing Co., 626 Broadway.] A.·. M.·. 5632, [1872.] 861 p. 8°. [Copyright, 1871.]

Rubricated title page.

MORALS AND DOGMA OF THE ANCIENT AND ACCEPTED SCOTTISH RITE OF FREEMASONRY. Prepared [By Albert Pike] for the Supreme Council of the Thirty-Third Degree, for the Southern Jurisdiction of the United States, and published by its authority. New York, Robert Macoy, 4 Barclay street, 1878, 861 p. 8°.

Rubricated title page.

Some copies of this edition were divided into four parts and bound in paper covers, separate title pages to each part, the first: Lodge of perfection; second: Chapter of Rose Croix; third: Council of Kadosh; fourth: Consistory. Rubricated title pages.

MORALS AND DOGMA OF THE ANCIENT AND ACCEPTED SCOTTISH RITE OF FREEMASONRY. Prepared [By Albert Pike] for the Supreme Council of the Thirty-Third Degree, for the Southern Jurisdiction of the United States, and published by its authority. Charleston, [New York?] A.·. M.·. 5641, [1881.] 861 p. 8°.

MORALS AND DOGMA OF THE ANCIENT AND ACCEPTED SCOTTISH RITE OF FREEMASONRY. Prepared [By Albert Pike] for the Supreme Council of the Thirty-Third Degree, for the Southern Jurisdiction of the United States, and published by its authority. Charleston, [Washington, George E. Howard & Co.] A.·. M.·. 5641, [1881.] [Copyright, 1906.] 861 p. 8°.

Rubricated title page.

New Age, v. 4, no. 3, March 1906, p. 257 [presumably by Grand Commander George Fleming Moore]: "The Supreme Council for the Southern Jurisdiction . . . has just published a new and improved edition . . . no changes have been made in the meaning, nor in the words, and even the very paging of the former editions has been preserved. But . . . numerous typographical and other similar errors have been corrected."

MORALS AND DOGMA OF THE ANCIENT AND ACCEPTED SCOTTISH RITE OF FREEMASONRY. Prepared [By Albert Pike] for the Supreme Council of the Thirty-Third Degree, for the Southern Jurisdiction of the United States, and published by its authority. Charleston, [Manufactured by L. H. Jenkins, Inc., Richmond, Va., May, 1918.] A.˙. M.˙. 5641, [1881.] 861 p. 8°.

Rubricated title. The above editions of this work are printed from stereotyped plates.
Transactions, 1919, 133: "Plates about used up. Edition now being made is last [from these plates]."
New plates and large supply of new printing reported on hand in 1921.
Transactions, 1923-1925, 147: reports "new edition" of better paper and binding, including the Hugo Digest Index.
Reprinted as needed after 1927, with "Esoteric" paragraph added in 1947.

OFFICES OF CONSECRATION AND DEDICATION OF A TEMPLE OR HALL OF THE ANCIENT AND ACCEPTED SCOTTISH RITE OF FREEMASONRY IN THE SOUTHERN JURISDICTION, U. S. A. [By Albert Pike.] Gr[and] Or[ient] of Charleston, 1886. 26 p. 8°.

Probably printed in Washington.
Reprinted, 1924.

OFFICES OF CONSECRATION AND DEDICATION OF THE HOUSE OF THE TEMPLE OF THE SUPREME COUNCIL OF THE 33D DEGREE OF THE ANCIENT AND ACCEPTED SCOTTISH RITE OF FREEMASONRY, FOR THE SOUTHERN JURISDICTION, U. S. A. [By Albert Pike.] At the orient of Washington, October 22, 1884. 23 p. 8°.

OFFICES OF CONSECRATION OF A HALL OF FREEMASONS OF THE ANCIENT AND ACCEPTED SCOTTISH RITE IN THE SOUTHERN JURISDICTION OF THE UNITED STATES. [By Albert Pike.] Or[ient] of Charleston, A.˙. M.˙. 5635. Washington, D. C., printed by Judd & Detweiler, 1875. 16 p. 8°.

OFFICE OF CONSTITUTION AND INAUGURATION OF A LODGE OF PERFECTION, AND INSTALLATION OF ITS OFFICERS, [By Albert Pike] as used in the Southern Jurisdiction of the United States. 'lepodoy. [New York?] A.˙. M.˙. 5630, [1870.] 92 p. 8°.

Copyright 1872. There are two title pages. The first one reads: "Offices of inauguration and installation of the Ancient and Accepted Scottish Rite, as used in the Southern Jurisdiction of the United States. A.˙.M.˙. 5630."

OFFICES OF CONSTITUTION AND INAUGURATION OF A LODGE OF PERFECTION, AND INSTALLATION OF ITS OFFICERS, [By Albert Pike] as used in the Southern Jurisdiction of the United States. New edition. Or[ient] of Charleston [New York.] 5643 [1883.] 78 p. 8°.

OFFICES OF CONSTITUTION AND INAUGURATION OF A COUNCIL OF PRINCES OF JERUSALEM, AND INSTALLATION OF ITS DIGNITARIES AND OFFICERS, [By Albert Pike] as used in the Southern Jurisdiction of the United States. 'lepodoy. [New York?] A.˙. M.˙. 5630 [1870.] 86 p. 2 plates. 8°.

Copyright 1872.

OFFICES OF CONSTITUTION AND INAUGURATION OF A CHAPTER OF KNIGHTS ROSE CROIX OF HIERODOM, AND INSTALLATION OF ITS DIGNITARIES AND OFFICERS, [By Albert Pike] as used in the Southern Jurisdiction of the United States. 'lepodoy. [New York?] A.˙. M.˙. 5630 [1870.] 60 p. 2 plates. 8°.

OFFICES OF CONSTITUTION AND INAUGURATION OF A COUNCIL OF KNIGHTS KADOSH, AND INSTALLATION OF ITS OFFICERS, [By Albert Pike] as used in the Southern Jurisdiction of the United States. 'lepodoy. [New York?] [about 1870.] 87 p. 3 plates. 8°.

[OFFICES OF] CONSTITUTION AND INAUGURATION OF GRAND AND PARTICULAR CONSISTORIES OF SUBLIME PRINCES, [By Albert Pike], 1870.

Copy unlocated, but title was advertised in *Official Bulletin*, I, Part 2, August 1870, p. 139; and again in VII, 1885, p. 502.

OFFICES OF CONSTITUTION AND INAUGURATION OF A CONSISTORY OF THE 32D DEGREE. [By Albert Pike.] [N. p. N. d.] 76 p. 8°.

Transactions, 1937, 34/35 reports revised and reprinted for all four Bodies in 1936.

OFFICES OF MASONIC BAPTISM, RECEPTION OF A LOUVETEAU, AND ADOPTION. Prepared [By Albert Pike] for the Supreme Council, 33°, for the Southern Jurisdiction of the United States. 'lepodoy. [New York?] A.'. M.'. 5631 [1871.] Illus. 70+70+74 p. 8°.

OFFICIA SUPREMA AT THE OBSEQUIES OF A KNIGHT KADOSH.

See Ceremonies at the obsequies of a Knight Kadosh.

[HEBREW TEXT.] The porch and the middle chamber. . . The book of the lodge [by Albert Pike.] 'lepodoy. [New York?] A.'. M.'. 5632 [1872.] 343 p. 8°. Illus.

Rubricated title page.

[HEBREW TEXT] OR, THE INNER SANCTUARY. [By Albert Pike.] Part First. The book of the Lodge of Perfection. Latomopolis [New York?] A.'. M.'. 5621 [1861.] 280 p. 8°.

Rubricated title page.

THE INNER SANCTUARY. [By Albert Pike.] Part I. The book of the Lodge of Perfection. 'lepodoy. [New York?] A.'. M.'. 5630 [1870.] 315 p. 8°.

Rubricated title page.

THE INNER SANCTUARY. [By Albert Pike.] Part I. The book of the Lodge of Perfection. Or[ient] of Charleston [New York?] A.'. M.'. 5643 [1883.] 290 p. 8°.

Rubricated title page.

DER INNERE TEMPEL. [By Albert Pike.] Erster theil. Das buch der Loge der Vollkommenheit. 'lepodoy. [New York?] A.'. M.'. 5630 [1870.] 242 p. 8°.

Transactions, 1882, Appendix p. 13, indicates printing in or after 1880; 1905, 123: Plates last used, May 1884.

[HEBREW TEXT] THE INNER SANCTUARY. [By Albert Pike] Part II. Latomopolis. A.'. M.'. 5621 [1861] 71 p. 8°.

THE INNER SANCTUARY. [By Albert Pike.] Part II. The book of the second temple. [New York?] A.'. M.'. 5630 [1870.] 109 p. 8°.

[HEBREW TEXT] THE INNER SANCTUARY. [By Albert Pike] Part II. The book of the Second Temple. 'lepodoy A.'. M.'. 5642 [1882] 109 p. 8°.

[HEBREW TEXT] OR THE INNER SANCTUARY [by Albert Pike.] Part III. Latomopolis [New York?] A.'. M.'. 5621 [1861.] 144 p. 8°.

Rubricated title page.

[HEBREW TEXT] OR THE INNER SANCTUARY [by Albert Pike.] Part III. [New York?] A.·. M.·. 5630 [1870.] 154 p. 8°.

Rubricated title page.
Revision with corrections commenced in 1927 and marked "Reprinted 1937." German *Das Buch Von Zweiter Temple: Transactions*, 1884, Appendix, p. 46, show rituals in German 4° to 18° printed; 1905, 123: Plates last used March 1887.

[HEBREW TEXT] THE INNER SANCTUARY [By Albert Pike] Parts II and III . . . [Baltimore] A.·.M.·. 5717. 1957. 296 p.

In this edition unfamiliar names in printed form, but not those in code, have been Anglicized. Includes explanatory material not by Pike.

THE INNER SANCTUARY. [By Albert Pike.] Part IV. The book of the Holy House. [New York?] A.·. M.·. 5627 [1867.] 553 p. 8°.

Rubricated title page.

THE INNER SANCTUARY. [By Albert Pike.] Part IV. The book of the Holy House. [New York?] A.·. M.·. 5644 [1884.] 487 p. 8°.

THE INNER SANCTUARY. [By Albert Pike.] Part V. The book of the Holy House. [New York?] A.·. M.·. 5627 [1867.] 296 p. 8°.

Rubricated title page.

RITUAL. [By Albert Pike.] Part V. The inner sanctuary. The book of the great Light. [New York, J. J. Little & Co., 10 to 20 Astor Place.] A.·. M.·. 5639 [1879.] 141 p. 8°.

Colored plates and illustrations.
"Copyright 1879." Only copyrighted ritual.

RITUAL. [By Albert Pike.] Part V. The inmost sanctuary. The book of the Great Light. 'lepodoy. A.·. M.·. 5643 [1882] 141 p. 8°.

No color plates.

[TWENTY-FIFTH DEGREE:]
I°. Book. House of the Earth. 8 p.
II°. Book. House of the Planets. 8 p.
III°. Book. House of the Sun and Moon. 5 p.
IV°. Book. House of the Light. 5 p.

All by Albert Pike. Wide 8°, N. p. N. d. Cover titles.

ANCIENT AND ACCEPTED SCOTTISH RITE. Thirty-first and thirty-second degrees. By Ill.·. Bros. Albert Pike, 33d and Charles Laffon DeLadebat, 33d, Active members of the Supreme Council for the Southern Jurisdiction of the United States of America, sitting at Charleston, S. C. New Orleans, 1858. 48+68 p. 8°.

First printed ritual adopted by Supreme Council in 1860.

[ESOTERIC WORK OF THE 1-3°, ACCORDING TO THE ANCIENT AND ACCEPTED SCOTTISH RITE. By Albert Pike.] N. p. N. d. 43 p. 4°.

[ESOTERIC WORK OF THE 1-3°, ACCORDING TO THE ANCIENT AND ACCEPTED SCOTTISH RITE. By Albert Pike.] N. p. N. d. 16 p. 12°.

[ESOTERIC WORK OF THE IV-XIV°. By Albert Pike. Washington?] N. d. 36+2 p. 8°.

[ESOTERIC WORK OF THE IV-XIV°. By Albert Pike.] Supreme Council Press, 1909. 36 p. 8°.

B I B L I O G R A P H Y

[Geheime Arbeit. IV-XIV. By Albert Pike] 38 p. 8°.

Title taken from bound cover. N.p. N.d.
Rubricated title page.

[Esoteric work of the XV-XVIII°. By Albert Pike. Washington?] N. d. 45+2 p. 8°.

[Esoteric work of the XV-XVIII°. By Albert Pike.] Supreme Council Press, A.·. M.·. 5665 [1905] 45 p. 8°.

[Esoteric work of the XV-XVIII°. By Albert Pike. Baltimore] 1957. 64 p.

[The esoteric work of the XIX-XXX°. By Albert Pike. Washington?] N. d. 28+2 p. 8°.

[The esoteric work of the XIX-XXX°. By Albert Pike. Supreme Council Press, A.·. M.·. 5667 (1907)] 28 p. 8°.

[The esoteric work of the XXXI-XXXII°. By Albert Pike. Washington? about 1879.] 24+3 p. 8°.

[The esoteric work of the XXXI-XXXII°. By Albert Pike. Washington, Supreme Council Press, A.·. M.·. 5667 (1907)]. 24 p. 8°.

Note: Previous to 1880 all secret work was copied in manuscript. In that year the esoteric material was printed for the first time [*Transactions*, 1880, Appendix, p. 6] and is therefore the probable imprint date.

Legenda of the Lodge of Perfection, Southern Jurisdiction, U. S. A. [By Albert Pike.] Charleston, [Washington?] 1888. 43 p. 8°.

Same. N. p. 1921. 43 p. 8°.

Legenda. [By Albert Pike.] XIX-XXX°. [N. p. 1884?] 170 p. 8°.

XXXII°. Legenda [A] [By Albert Pike.] [N. d., about 1880?]. 42 p. 8°.

XXXII°. Legenda B. [By Albert Pike.] [N. p. 1880?] 23 p. 8°.

XXXII°. Legenda [A]-B. [By Albert Pike.] [N. p. 1880?] 42+23 p. 8°.

Readings. XXXII°. [By Albert Pike.] [N. p. 1880?] 162 p. 8°.

The book of the words. [Sephar h'debarim.] [N. p.] A.·. M.·. 5638. [1878] 176. 4 p., Wide 8°.

Edition limited to 150 copies. Explanatory of words in the rituals.

Music for the ritual of the various degrees in the Ancient and Accepted Scottish Rite of Freemasonry, according to the working of the Mother Council of the World, (S.J.U.S.A.), selected, arranged and composed by Matthew Cooke.

Part I [with Preface by Albert Pike]. Gr.·. Orient of Charleston A.·. M.·. 5641 [1881] xix, 168p.

Part II. Gr.·. Orient of Charleston, A.·. M.·. 5641 [1881] pp. 169-507.

Part III. Gr.·. Orient of Charleston, A.·. M.·. 5641 [1881] pp. 508-617.

Part IV. Gr.·. Orient of Charleston, A.·. M.·. 5641 [1881] pp. 618-751.

All printed at New York by J. J. Little & Co., copyrighted by Albert Pike, 1880.

MISCELLANEOUS

ALBERT PIKE ON BLUE LODGE MASONRY. *In* Trestle Board, v. 17, no. 8, February, 1904, p. 296.

ALBERT PIKE ON PRAYER. *In* Trestle Board, v. 15, no. 2, August, 1901.

ANCIENT AND ACCEPTED SCOTTISH RITE OF FREEMASONRY. The constitutions and regulations of 1762. Statutes and regulations of Perfection and other degrees. Vera instituta secreta et fundamenta ordinis of 1786. The secret constitutions of the 33d degree, with the statutes of 1859, 1866, 1868, 1870 and 1872, of the Supreme Council for the Southern Jurisdiction. Compiled by Albert Pike, Sovereign Grand Commander of the Supreme Council of the 33d degree for the Southern Jurisdiction of the United States. New York, Masonic Publishing Company, No. 626 Broadway, A. M. 5632. [1872] 467 p. 4°.

Same. 8°.
Rubricated title pages to both above editions.
Addenda 207/211 issued 2/1/1883.

ANCIENT AND ACCEPTED SCOTTISH RITE OF FREEMASONRY. The constitutions and regulations of 1762. Statutes and regulations of Perfection, and other degrees. Vera instituta secreta et fundamenta ordinis of 1786. The secret constitutions of the 33d degree, with the statutes of 1859, 1866, 1868, 1870, and 1872, of the Supreme Council for the Southern Jurisdiction. Compiled by Albert Pike, Sovereign Grand Commander of the Supreme Council of the 33d degree for the Southern Jurisdiction of the United States. New York, Masonic Publishing Company, A. M. 5632. [1872] New edition printed by J. J. Little & Co., 5664. [1904] 467 p. 8°.

Rubricated title page.
The Latin constitutions of 1786. Re-translated from the Latin. *In* New Age Magazine, v. 5, no. 3, Sept., 1906, p. 273-279; v. 6, no. 1, Jan., 1907, p. 81; no. 2, Feb., 1907, p. 187.

BAAL AND AUN. *See* Holy (The) Triad.

BALUSTRE OF THE SOVEREIGN GRAND COMMANDER [ALBERT PIKE] ON CERTAIN FOREIGN RELATIONS. *In* Supreme Council, Southern Jurisdiction, Transactions, 1868, p. 147-188.

GOULEY, GEORGE FRANK. Charges and specifications against. *In* Supreme Council, Southern Jurisdiction, Transactions, 1868, p. 69-74.

THE CHRISTIAN MYSTERIES. *In* Brownell, J. H. Gems from the quarry, v. 2, p. 151-152.

DECISIONS ON MASONIC LAW REGULATING REJECTIONS FOR MEMBERSHIP IN THE FRATERNITY. By Albert Pike. *In* New Age Magazine, v. 10, no. 1, January, 1908, p. 92-96.

THE DECISIONS OF THE SUPREME COUNCIL [ETC.] *See* The Supreme Council, 33d degree and the blue degrees.

BIBLIOGRAPHY

DEGREES ARE LESSONS. *In* Voice of Masonry, v. 27, no. 8, August, 1889, p. 700-702.

THE DUTIES OF FREEMASONRY. *In* Trestle Board, v. 8, no. 4, April, 1894, p. 145-151.

FATE AND CHANGE. *In* Brownell, J. H. Gems from the quarry, v. 1, p. 423.

FELLOWSHIP, *In* Brownell, J. H. Gems from the quarry, v. 1, p. 434; v. 2, p. 433-434.

FREEMASONRY [MEANING OF.] *In* Voice of Masonry, v. 22, no. 3, March, 1884, p. 192-195.

FREEMASONRY HAS ITS FAULTS. *In* Brownell, J. H. Gems from the quarry, v. 1, p. 434.

FREEMASONRY IS TOLERANCE. *In* Square & Compass, v. 4, no. 3, May, 1895, p. 61-63.

GNOSTICISM, THE KABBALA, AND THE MYSTERIES, AS CONNECTED WITH AND ILLUSTRATING MASONRY. Nos. 1-5. *In* American Quarterly Review of Freemasonry, v. 1, p. 14-38, 160-191, 368-407, 448-460; v. 2, p. 19-33, 162-178, 313-335, 448-467.

GORGAS, FERDINAND, J. S., CHAIRMAN OF COMMITTEE OF FOREIGN CORRESPONDENCE VS. THE GRAND ORIENT OF FRANCE AND THE UNION OF GERMANIC GRAND LODGES. [Washington, 188—.] 8 p. 8°.

Signed: ‡ (that is, Albert Pike).

A GREAT BROTHERHOOD. *In* Brownell, J. H. Gems from the quarry, v. 1, p. 189.

GREAT IDEAS IN MYSTERIES. *In* Voice of Masonry, v. 35, no. XI, November, 1897, p. 803-825.

THE HOLY TRIAD . . JAH: BAAL-PEOR, THE SYRIAN PRIAPUS: THE CITY OF IDOLATRY AND INIQUITY. A reply to the Grand Chaplain and Grand High Priest of the Grand Royal Arch Chapter of Massachusetts. (From Mackey's National Freemason.) Washington City, office of Mackey's National Freemason, 1873. 34 p. 8°.

Signed: Albert Pike.
Same, entitled "Baal and Aun." *In* Mackey's National Freemason, v. 2, Sep., 1873, p. 626-657.

HUMANITY. *In* Brownell, J. H. Gems from the quarry, v. 1, p. 372.

INDIVIDUAL RESPONSIBILITY. *In* Brownell, J. H. Gems from the quarry, v. 2, p. 468.

LECTURE ON MASONIC SYMBOLISM. [By Albert Pike.] Gloria dei est celare verbum. [New York? about 1875.] Illus. 188 p. 4°.

Probably printed by Lange, Little & Co., who printed his "Second lecture." 100 copies only printed and distributed to 32nds or 33rds, who had contributed towards the expense of its publication, and Pike enjoined "That this volume shall never be sold or otherwise disposed of."

A SECOND LECTURE ON SYMBOLISM. The Omkara and other ineffable words. [By Albert Pike.] [New York, Lang, Little & Co., printers.] [about 1876.] Illus. 292 p. 4°.

100 copies only printed. Intended as the complement of his "Lecture on masonic symbolism."

A LETTER TOUCHING MASONIC SYMBOLISM. 10 p. 8°. Caption title.

Signed: Albert Pike, Washington, 8th November, 1889.
The letter is to Robert Freke Gould, the celebrated masonic historian of England.
Same in his Official Bulletins, v. 10, p. 306-312.

LIFE. *In* Brownell, J. H. Gems from the quarry, v. 1, p. 302.

LIGHT AGAINST DARKNESS. *In* Brownell, J. H. Gems from the quarry, v. 2, p. 238.

LIVERY COMPANIES OR GUILDS. *In* Mackey's National Freemason, v. 1, April, 1872, p. 339-352.

MASONIC (THE) AND PATRIOTIC FEAST TO BRO. THE GEN. LAFAYETTE, SOV. G. INSP. G. 33D DEG., by the lodges of the French and Scottish Rites, united, October 10, 1830. Translated from the French for the American Freemason, by M. W. Bro. Albert Pike, of Arkansas. *In* American Freemason of Louisville, Ky., v. 3, nos. 5-8, December, 1854, January, 1855, p. 34, 42, 50, 58.

MASONIC GEMS. *In* Voice of Masonry, v. 19, no. 3, March, 1881, p. 196-198.

MASONIC JUSTICE. *In* Trestle Board, v. 7, no. 6, June, 1893, p. 245-250.

MASONIC TRIALS. *In* New Age Magazine, v. 9, no. 6, December, 1908, p. 575-580. From decisions in Supreme Council Transactions of 1880, p. 28.

MASONIC VIEWS OF CHRISTIANITY. *In* American Freemasons Magazine, v. 5, January 9, 1860, p. 43-45.

MASONRY (THE) OF ADOPTION. [By Albert Pike.] N. p. [1866] [234] p.
Same. [EXTRACTS] *In* Masonic Eclectic (New York), v. 3, no. 1, November, 1867, p. 332-338.

MATERIALS FOR THE HISTORY OF FREEMASONRY IN FRANCE AND ELSEWHERE ON THE CONTINENT OF EUROPE, FROM 1718 TO 1859. By Albert Pike, 33° . . v. 1, A.·. M.·. 5636, [1876.] 78 p. 8°.

The beginning of this work, which was to be published from time to time in his Official Bulletins, the "Vol. 1," being additional pages 1-78 of his Official Bulletins, v. 3, no. 2, July, 1876.
See also his Manuscripts.

MATERIALS FOR THE HISTORY OF FREEMASONRY IN FRANCE. [By Albert Pike.] Edited, arranged and annotated by George F. Moore. *In* New Age Magazine, v. 1, no. 6, December, 1904, p. 577-594; v. 2, nos. 1, 2, 3, 4, 5, January, February, March, April, May, 1905, p. 61-73, 165-177, 259-271, 347-360, 429-438; v. 3, nos. 1-6, July-December, 1905, p. 55-66, 157-165, 251-261, 349-355, 449-457, 549-556; v. 4, nos. 1-6, January-June, 1906, p. 49-58, 149-157, 249-257, 349-357,

449-456, 549-555; v. 5, nos. 1-6, July-December, 1906, p. 49-56, 145-152, 241-244, 335-340, 433-439, 531-539; v. 6, nos. 1-6, January-June, 1907, p. 49-55, 147-152, 245-250, 343-348, 441-447, 539-545; v. 7, nos. 1-3, 5, 6, July-September, November, December, 1907, p. 49-55, 147-153, 243-249, 435-441, 531-535; v. 8, nos. 1-6, January-June, 1908, p. 49-56, 145-150, 251-254, 347-353, 441-445, 537-542; v. 9, nos. 1-4, July-October, 1908, p. 49-54, 144-148, 241-244, 341-345; v. 10, no. 6, June, 1909, p. 540-543; v. 11, nos. 1-4, July-October, 1909, p. 55-58, 145-149, 272-276, 337-341.

Embodying about all of v. 1 of his Manuscripts on the subject.

NECESSITY OF STUDY TO A MASON. *In* Masonic Eclectic (New York), v. 1, no. 1, September, 1860, p. 33-34.

THE NINE GREAT TRUTHS IN MASONRY. *In* American Quarterly Review of Freemasonry, v. 1, p. 80-85; Voice of Masonry, v. 27, no. 3, March, 1889, p. 202-207.

OCCASIONAL BULLETINS OF THE SUPREME COUNCIL FOR THE SOUTHERN JURISDICTION OF THE UNITED STATES. [Compiled and edited by Albert Pike.]

No. 1, December, 1887. [Washington.] 3 p. 8°.

No. 2, March, 1888. [Washington.] 17 p. 8°.

Another edition: No. 2, March, 1888. [Washington.] 31 p. 8°. P. 17-31 of this edition contain the same subject matter as the first copy.

No. 3, April, 1888. 9 p. 8°.
No. 4, May, 1888. 12 p. 8°.
No. 5, June, 1888. 48 p. 8°.
No. 6, July, 1888. 48 p. 8°.
No. 7, September, 1888. 33 p. 8°.
No. 8, April, 1889. 56 p. 8°.
No. 9, July, 1889. 91 p. 8°.
Supplement, July, 1889. 8 p. 8°.
No. 10, January, 1890. 113 p. 8°.
No. 11, March, 1891. 61 p. 8°.
No. 12, May, 1891. 101 p. 8°.

These Bulletins were all probably printed in Washington. No. 12 appeared after Pike's death in April, 1891.

OFFICIAL BULLETINS OF THE SUPREME COUNCIL OF THE 33RD DEGREE FOR THE SOUTHERN JURISDICTION OF THE UNITED STATES. [Compiled and edited by Albert Pike.]

Vol. 1, no. 1, May, 1870. Charleston. [Masonic Publishing Co., 432 Broome street, New York.] p. 1-56 8°. Some copies of this number are printed: "For the Southern and Northern Jurisdiction," and contain the imprint: "Charleston and Boston."

No. 2, August, 1870. Charleston [Masonic Publishing Co., New York.] p. 57-138 8°.

No. 3, April, 1871. Charleston [Masonic Publishing Co., New York.] p. 139-326 8°.

No. 4, December, 1871. Charleston [Masonic Publishing Co., 626 Broadway, New York.] p. 327-548 8°.

No. 5, June, 1872. Charleston [Masonic Publishing Co., 626 Broadway, New York.] p. 549-660.

Vol. 2, No. 1, August, 1872. Charleston [Union Printing Co., 79 John street, New York.] 218 p. 8°.

No. 2, April, 1873. Charleston [Union Printing Co., 79 John street, New York.] 244 p. 8°. Cover title "June, 1873," as date.

No. 3, August, 1874. Charleston [Masonic Publishing Co., 626 Broadway, New York.] 205 p. 8°. Cover title says "January, 1875."

Vol. 3, No. 1, January, 1875. Charleston [New York. Lange, Little & Co., printers, No. 10 to 20 Astor Place.] p. 1-320 8°.

No. 2, July, 1876. Charleston [New York. Lange, Little & Co., printers, No. 10 to 20 Astor Place.] p. 321-350 8°. Additional pages 1-78, containing "Materials for the history of freemasonry in France and elsewhere on the continent of Europe, from 1718 to 1859. By Albert Pike, 33° [etc.] Nos. 1 and 2 were issued at the same time, in the same wrapper or covers.

No. [3], March, 1878, Gr[and] Orient of Charleston [New York. J. J. Little & Co., printers, 10 to 20 Astor Place.] p. 351-686 8°. Called "No. 2," should be "No. 3." Cover title says, "April, 1878."

Vol. 4, No. 1, January 1, 1880. Charleston [New York?] p. 1-392 8°. Cover title says "April, 1880."

Nos. 2, 3, February, 1881, Charleston [New York?] p. 393-738, index p. 1-7, books p. 1-3.

Vol. 5, No. 1, July, 1882. Charleston. p. 1-415 8°.

No. 2, September, 1883. Charleston. p. 416-653, index 24 p. Cover title says "October, 1883."

Vol. 6, No. 1, April, 1884. Gr[and] Or[ient] of Charleston. p. 1-535 8°. Cover title says, "May, 1884."

No. 2, July, 1884, Gr[and] Or[ient] of Charleston, p. 536-651. Index 18 p. 8°.

Vol. 7, No. 1, April, 1885. Gr[and] Or[ient] of Charleston, p. 1-519. 8°. Cover title says "July, 1885."

No. 2, March, 1886. Gr[and] Or[ient] of Charleston, p. 520-824, index 20 p. Cover title says "June, 1886."

Vol. 8, No. 1, September, 1887. Gr[and] Or[ient] of Charleston, p. 1-332, supplemental pages 1-54, containing Allocution of the Grand Commander, session of 1886.

No. 2, September, 1888. Gr[and] Or[ient] of Charleston, p. 333-748, index 21 p. 8°. Cover title says "October, 1888."

Vol. 9, No. 1, March, 1889. Gr[and] Or[ient] of Charleston, p. 1-339 8°. Cover title says "April, 1889."

No. 2, October, 1889. Gr[and] Or[ient] of Charleston, p. 340-647, index 22 p. 8°.

Vol. 10, No. 1, June, 1890. Gr[and] Or[ient] of Charleston. p. 1-404 8°.

No. 2, June, 1892. Gr[and] Orient of Charleston, p. 405-845, index 22 p.

BIBLIOGRAPHY.

A PLEA FOR ARBITRATION. *In* Brownell, J. H. Gems from the quarry, v. 1, p. 335-336; Voice of Masonry, v. 27, no. 4, April, 1889, p. 308-310.

PRESTIGE OF MASONRY. *In* Trestle Board, v. 5, no. 10, October, 1891, p. 437-440.

THE REGIUS MANUSCRIPT. 8p. 8°. Caption title.

Signed: Albert Pike, Washington, 26th September, 1889.

Same in his Official Bulletins, v. 9, p. 637-644; Voice of Masonry, v. 28, no. 2, Feb., 1890, p. 94-99; Freemason's Repository, v. 19, no. 7, April, 1890, p. 348-355.

A REPLY FOR THE ANCIENT AND ACCEPTED SCOTTISH RITE OF FREEMASONRY [By Albert Pike] to the encyclical letter "Humanum Genus" of Pope Leo XIII, against freemasonry and the spirit of the age. Charleston, [Washington.] July, 1884. 40 p. 8°.

The first edition.

A REPLY FOR THE ANCIENT AND ACCEPTED SCOTTISH RITE OF FREEMASONRY [By Albert Pike] to the encyclical letter "Humanum Genus" of Pope Leo XIII. Charleston [Washington.] July, 1884. 37 p. 8°.

A REPLY FOR THE ANCIENT AND ACCEPTED SCOTTISH RITE OF FREEMASONRY [By Albert Pike] to the letter "Humanum Genus" of Pope Leo XIII. Gr[and] Or[ient] of Charleston [Washington] 1884. 48 p. 8°.

A REPLY FOR THE ANCIENT AND ACCEPTED SCOTTISH RITE OF FREEMASONRY [By Albert Pike] to the letter "Humanum Genus" of Pope Leo XIII. Gr[and] Orient of Charleston [Washington] 1884. 59 p. 8°.

Same in Masonic Home Journal, v. 2, nos. 9, 12-14, 16-18, 1884-85, p. 70, 98, 105, 113, 129, 137, 145.

Same in his Official Bulletins, v. 6, p. 542-576.

Same in same, v. 7, p. 39-76.

Pages 49-59 of this edition contain extracts from "Profession of faith of the XIXth century," by Eugene Pelletan.

THE LETTER "HUMANUM GENUS" OF THE POPE, LEO XIII, AGAINST FREEMASONRY AND THE SPIRIT OF THE AGE, APRIL 20, 1884, AND THE REPLY FOR THE ANCIENT AND ACCEPTED SCOTTISH RITE OF FREEMASONRY [By Albert Pike.] Gr[and] Orient of Charleston, [Washington] 1884. 37+59 p. 8°. Cover title.

Pages 1-37, original text and translation of the "Letter."

THE LETTER "HUMANUM GENUS" OF THE POPE, LEO XIII, AGAINST FREEMASONRY AND THE SPIRIT OF THE AGE, APRIL 20, 1884, AND THE REPLY FOR THE ANCIENT AND ACCEPTED SCOTTISH RITE OF FREEMASONRY [By Albert Pike.] Gr[and] Orient of Charleston, [Washington] 1884. 42+70 p. 8°. Cover title.

Reprinted in 1948.

P. 1-42 contain the original text and translation of the "Letter." P. 57-70 contain extracts from "Profession of faith of the XIXth century," by Eugene Pelletan.

Same, extracts, entitled "Humanity's great foe." *In* Brownell, J. H. Gems from the quarry, v. 1, p. 254-273; Masonic Review, v. 63, no. 4, May, 1885, p. 193-196; Texas Freemason, Nov. and Dec., 1884, Jan.-April, 1885, p. 29-32, 87-91, 121-125, 159-167, 192-194. Voice of Masonry, v. 22, no. 10, Oct., 1884, p. 846-963, v. 23, no. 6, June, 1885, p. 498-504.

This "Reply" of Pike's was translated into Spanish and published in Cuba, and into Italian and published at Rome. (From his Official Bulletins, v. 7, p. 283.)

ALBERT PIKE

THE SEVEN LIGHTS. A reading. [By Albert Pike.] [Washington] Jos. L. Pearson, printer [188—.] 25 p. 8°.

Another edition lacking the printer's imprint at the end.

THE STATUTES AND REGULATIONS, INSTITUTES, LAWS, AND GRAND CONSTITUTIONS OF THE ANCIENT AND ACCEPTED SCOTTISH RITE. Compiled with notes, from authentic documents, for the use of the order. By Albert Pike, 33d, M.·. P.·. Sovereign Grand Commander of the Supreme Council for the Southern Jurisdiction of the United States. New York, Robert Macoy, publisher, 1859. 168 p. 4°.

Same. 8°.
Rubricated title page.

THE SUPREME COUNCIL, 33D, AND THE BLUE DEGREES. Question of jurisdiction. Washington, L. G. Stephens & Son, printers, 1879. 18 p. 8°.

Signed: Albert Pike.

Same, entitled The decisions of the Supreme Council of the 33d degree for the Southern Jurisdiction of the United States in regard to the right of Supreme Councils to administer the blue degrees. Washington, Jos. L. Pearson, printer, 1889. 18 p. 8°.

Same, entitled "Control of the blue degrees." *In* Voice of Masonry, v. 22, no. 1, Jan., 1884, p. 71-77.

THE TAU AND THE TRIPLE TAU. *In* Square & Compass, v. 17, no. 8, October, 1908, p. 198-200.

TEMPLARISM, ITS DUTY AND ITS SPHERE. *In* Brownell, J. H. Gems from the quarry, v. 1, p. 128-129; Masonic Eclectic, v. 1, no. 10, April, 1877, p. 438-440.

THE TEMPLARS, A SKETCH. *In* American Quarterly Review of Freemasonry, v. 1, January, 1858, p. 307, 319.

THE TETRAGRAMMATON. *In* Mackey's National Freemason, v. 2, March, 1873, p. 296-302.

THOUGHTS AND ACTIONS. *In* Brownell, J. H. Gems from the quarry, v. 2, p. 486.

VINDICATION OF THE ANCIENT AND ACCEPTED SCOTTISH RITE [By Albert Pike] against certain libels. (From the Memphis Appeal, as published in 1867.) Washington, Cunningham & McIntosh, printers, 1871. 93 p. 8°.

WHAT DOES FREEMASONRY TEACH? *In* Trestle Board, v. 6, no. 7, July, 1892, p. 289-298.

WHICH PAYS BEST? *In* Voice of Masonry, v. 27, no. 7, July, 1889, p. 599-601.

WHY FREEMASONRY EXISTS. *In* Voice of Masonry, v. 27, no. 5, May, 1889, p. 398-402.

WORTH AND FELLOWSHIP. *In* Voice of Masonry, v. 28, no. 9, September, 1890, p. 653-655.

B I B L I O G R A P H Y

THE ZODIAC SIGNS AND JACOB'S SONS. *In* Square & Compass, v. 15, no. 7, September, 1906, p. 180-181.

ZOROASTER OR ZARATHUSTRA, AND HIS DOCTRINES. *In* Mackey's National Freemason, v. 3, December, 1893, p. 117-122.

MANUSCRIPTS

[Account as Grand Commander of the Supreme Council, 33°, Southern Jurisdiction, Ancient and Accepted Scottish Rite of Freemasonry, from 1861 to 1878.]

Written in a Cash Book of 288 p. Some pages blank. Loosely inserted are 44 p. of accounts.

An address on the actions and character of John Anthony Quitman, Sovereign Grand Inspector General. [By Albert Pike.] 1860. 45 written pages. Wide 8°.

Each written page bordered in red ink. This is the MS. from which printed copies were made, appearing in the proceedings of the Supreme Council, for 1860, and also in separate pamphlet form. Not paged.

Address of the M. P. Sovereign Grand Commander [Albert Pike] to the Supreme Council for the Southern Jurisdiction of the United States, at its adjourned session, on the 5th day of the Heb.˙. month *Nisan* A. M. 5620 [1860.] 86 written pages. Wide 8°.

Other side of each sheet blank, both sides bordered in red. Not paged. The MS. from which the address in the Transactions of the Supreme Council for 1860 was printed. Bound with his address on John Anthony Quitman.

[Book of the words. By Albert Pike.] [N. d.] 350 written pages. Oblong 8°.

Fifteen illustrations. No lettering or title page, all pages ruled with a border of red. Paper of fine and heavy quality. Bound in full blue morocco. This is his MS. of his "Book of the words."

Ceremony of adoption of the child of a brother by a symbolic Lodge. Prepared by the Bro.˙. A[lbert] P[ike] 33°, 1858. [Followed by another title page:] Ceremony of adoption of the child of a brother by a Lodge of Perfection. Prepared by the Bro.˙. A[lbert] P[ike] 33°, 1858. 100 pages. Wide 8°.

All pages ruled with a border of red. Bound with his "Funeral Ceremony of a Knight Rose Croix."

Ceremony of baptism of the child of a brother by a Lodge of Perfection. Prepared by the Bro.˙. A[lbert] P[ike] 33°. [1870?] 76 p. Wide 8°.

All pages bordered in red. Bound with his "Funeral Ceremony of a Knight Rose Croix."

Ceremony of inauguration and installation of a Lodge of Perfection. [By Albert Pike.] [1870?] 51 p. Wide 8°.

All pages ruled with a border of red. Other "Ceremonies" are bound with this MS. and the volume lettered "Inaugurations and Installations." The other MSS. are noted in their proper places, with a reference to the first item in the volume.

[Ceremony of] Inauguration of a Council of Princes of Jerusalem. [By Albert Pike.] [1870?] 59 p. Wide 8°.

All pages ruled with a border of red. Bound with his "Ceremony of inauguration and installation of a Lodge of Perfection."

ALBERT PIKE

About 1878

CEREMONY OF INAUGURATION OF A CHAPTER OF ROSE CROIX. [By Albert Pike.] [1870?] 52 p. Wide 8°.

All pages ruled with a border of red. Bound with his "Ceremony of inauguration and installation of a Lodge of Perfection."

CEREMONY OF INAUGURATION OF A COUNCIL OF KADOSH, 30TH DEGREE. [By Albert Pike.] [1879?] 35 p. Wide 8°.

All pages ruled with a border of red. Bound with his "Ceremony of inauguration and installation of a Lodge of Perfection."

[CEREMONY OF] INAUGURATION AND INSTALLATION OF A GRAND CONSISTORY OF PRINCES OF THE ROYAL SECRET. [By Albert Pike.] [1870?] 66 p. Wide 8°.

All pages ruled with a border of red. Bound with his "Ceremony of inauguration and installation of a Lodge of Perfection."

CEREMONY OF RECEPTION OF A LOUVETEAU BY A SYMBOLIC LODGE. Prepared by the Bro.˙. A[lbert] P[ike] 33°. 1858. 115 p. Wide 8°.

All pages ruled with a border of red. Bound with his "Funeral ceremony of a Knight Rose Croix."

THE DEGREE OF MASTER MARK MASON. Being the work of the Gr[and] Council of Princes of Jerusalem of South Carolina, and the oldest work extant anywhere. From a MS. in the archives of the Supreme Council at Charleston. 34 p. Wide 8°.

On the other side of the title page "Copied by me this 8th day of May, 1858. Albert Pike, Sov.˙. Gr.˙. Insp.˙. Gen.˙. 33d degree." All pages ruled with a border of red. Not paged. Bound in full morocco, gilt edges. Other MSS, are bound with this item, the volume lettered on back "Rituals, Various." The other items are noted in their proper place, with a reference to this first MS.

EXCERPTA LATOMICA. [Compiled by Albert Pike.] [About 1870.] 294 written p. Wide 8°.

All pages ruled with a border of red, with occasional pen illustrations. Full bound in morocco. Gilt edges.

Extracts from writers on masonry and philosophical subjects connected therewith, of various authors, with occasional remarks by Pike.

FUNERAL CEREMONY OF A KNIGHT ROSE CROIX. [By Albert Pike.] [187—.] 37 p. Wide 8°.

All pages ruled with a border of red. Bound in with this MS. are others by Pike, the volume being lettered: "Funeral Ceremony, Ceremony of baptism, Reception of Louveteau, Ceremony of adoption."

GRAND MAITRE ECOSSAIS, OR SCOTTISH ELDER MASTER AND KNIGHT OF ST. ANDREW, being the fourth degree of Ramsay, or of La Regime Reformé in Rectifié of Dresden. From an old manuscript in English, without name or date, found by me in the archives of the Supreme Council at Charleston. 36 written p. Wide 8°.

On the other side of title page: "Correctly copied by me, May 7th, 1858, in substance. Albert Pike, Sov.˙. Gr.˙. Insp.˙. Gen.˙. 33d." All pages ruled with a border of red. Not paged. Bound with his "Degree of Master Mark Mason."

KNIGHT OF THE MEDITERRANEAN PASS. From an old manuscript in the archives of the Supreme Council at Charleston, South Carolina. 21 written p. Wide 8°.

On other side of title page: "Accurately copied by me this 4th day of May, A. D. 1858. Albert Pike, Sov.·. Gr.·. Insp.·. Gen.·. 33d." All pages ruled with a border of red. Bound with his "Degree of Master Mark Mason."

LYCÉE DU SECOND GRADE OU ASPIRANTE GENS D'ARMES DES A[MIS] DE LA N[ATURE] ET DES A[RTS] DU NORD ET DE CHARLESTON. Le 2me D.·. 10eme mois de la fondation 40,002. et de la 7e de la R-g-n-t-n. 1802. Commencé la 8eme année. 28 written p. Wide 8°.

On the other side of title page: "Translated by me May 4, 1858, from an old French MS. found by me in the archives of the Supreme Council at Charleston. Albert Pike. Sov.·. Gr.·. Insp.·. Gen.·. 33d." On the following page is the translation of the title: "Lyceum of the second degree, or Aspirant soldiery of the friends of nature and the arts of the North of Charleston. The second day of the 10th month of the year of the foundation 40,002 and of that of Regeneration, 1802. Commenced the 8th year."

All pages ruled with a border of red. Bound with his "Degree of Master Mark Mason."

[MASONIC PHILOSOPHY. By Albert Pike.] [187—?] 444 written pages, 13 illustrations. Oblong 8°.

Symbolism, mythology, mysteries, etymology, etc., etc., particularly in its relation to the Ancient and Accepted Scottish Rite of Freemasonry.

Bound in full morocco, without title. All pages ruled with a border of red, with much underscoring of words in red. Paper of fine and heavy quality.

MASONIC RITUALS. In hoc signo vinces. Spes mea in deo est. [Translated by Albert Pike in 1854 and 1855.] 889 written p. Royal 8°.

A beautiful example of the bookbinder's art. Bound in full morocco, tooled and inlaid with masonic emblems, front and back, edges of pages gilt, with masonic emblems tooled thereon. The book is lockable by means of two masonically designed locks, with key. Title page is handsomely lettered with many masonic devices thereon, by an artistic penman, probably E. B. MacGrotty, 33°, Hon.·. of Washington, and all the pages are ruled with a border of red. There are many blank pages in the volume in addition to the written pages.

MATERIALS FOR THE HISTORY OF FREEMASONRY IN FRANCE AND ELSEWHERE ON THE CONTINENT OF EUROPE, FROM 1718 TO 1859. By Albert Pike, 33°. A.·. M.·. 5636 [1876.] 6 v. 1,460 written pages. Wide 8°.

In heavy cardboard covers, not bound. Pike says, in Transactions of the Supreme Council for 1874, p. 23 of the Appendix that these were prepared before the Civil War.

Some portions of vol. 1 have been printed in his Official Bulletins and in the New Age Magazine, published by the Supreme Council, Southern Jurisdiction.

REGISTER OF ALBERT PIKE, 33D.·. SOVEREIGN GRAND INSPECTOR GENERAL FOR ARKANSAS, WEST TENNESSEE AND THE DISTRICT OF COLUMBIA, commenced the 20th of March, A. D. 1853. 875 p. Royal 8°.

The last entry is on page 611, October 1, 1864. Balance of pages blank. All pages ruled with a border of red. Some few pages here and there between pages 1 and 611, left blank. Bound in full red morocco, gilt edges. Paper of fine quality.

BIBLIOGRAPHY

RITUALS OF KNIGHT OF THE RED CROSS, KNIGHT TEMPLAR AND KNIGHT OF MALTA. 121 p. 8°.

On heavy ruled paper; all pages bordered in red. "From a manuscript in possession of Ill.˙. Bro.˙. A. G. Mackey, of about the year 1805, as other entries in the manuscript show. Accurately copied by me with occasional corrections of the grammar only, this 12th day of May, A. D. 1858. Albert Pike, K. T. &c., Sov.˙. Gd.˙. Insp.˙. Gen'l.˙. 33rd." Bound in full leather, gilt edges. Lettered on front cover: "Rituals R.˙. + .˙. K.˙. T.˙. and K.˙. of M.˙."

[RITUALS OF THE ANCIENT AND ACCEPTED SCOTTISH RITE OF FREEMASONRY, FROM THE FIRST TO THE THIRTY-SECOND DEGREES, INCLUSIVE. By Albert Pike.] 1866. 398 written p. Wide 8°.

The title page has only the following on it: "Deus meumque jus." Then follows a cut or picture of the 33° eagle, after which: "Ordo ab chao." All cut from some printed source and pasted on this page.

The title page is ruled with a border of red, green and purple, balance of pages with a border of red. Bound in full morocco, gilt edges, with no lettering on cover.

RITUALS. Rit Ancien et Accepté: Eighteenth degree. Rit Ancien et Accepté. Sovereign Prince Rose Croix. Also known as Sovereign Princes Freemasons of Heredom, or Knights of the Eagle and Pelican. From an ancient French manuscript, 1857.

On last page of MS: "Accurately translated by me from an old and very handsomely written MS. purchased in April, 1856, at the sale in Paris of the library of le F.˙. Astier, this 28th October, 1857. Albert Pike. Sov.˙. Insp.˙. Gen.˙. 33d."

THIRTIETH DEGREE. Rit Ancien et Accepté, or Scottish Masonry. Kadosch or Knight of the White and Black Eagle. Nec plus ultra. Dernier terme de l'Ecossisme. From an ancient French manuscript from the library of the Ill.˙. Bro. F. Astier, Paris.

On last page of MS: "A true translation of the MS. in French, purchased for me at the sale of the Ill.˙. Bro.˙. F. Astier, in April, 1856. This translation being made and completed this 8th day of October, A. D. 1857. Given at Little Rock, Arkansas. Albert Pike, Rose Croix; K-H.˙. S.˙. P.˙. R.˙. S.˙. 33d, Sov .˙. Insp.˙. Gen.˙."

CHEVALIER KADOSCH, OR KNIGHT OF THE BLACK EAGLE: Grand Inspector, Grand Inquisitor, and Grand Elu.

On last page of MS: "Accurately translated by me October, 1857, from a French MS. purchased at the sale of the library of the deceased Bro.˙. F. Astier, Paris, in 1856. Little Rock, Arkansas, Albert Pike, R.˙. Croix.˙. K-H.˙. S.˙. P.˙. R.˙. S.˙. & Sov.˙. Gen.˙. 33d."

THE FALSE KNIGHT KADOSCH, OR KADOSCH OF CROMWELL.

On last page: "Carefully translated by me from an old French MS. purchased for me at the sale of the library of the Ill.˙. Bro.˙. F. Astier, in Paris, in April, 1856. Albert Pike, Rose Croix.˙. S.˙.P.˙.R.˙.S.˙. Sov.˙. Gr.˙. Insp.˙. Gen.˙. 33d, 13th October, 1857."

THIRTY-SECOND DEGREE OF THE ANCIENT AND ACCEPTED SCOTTISH RITE. Sublime Prince of the Royal Secret. Truthful Guardian of the Sacred Treasure. Translated from an ancient French manuscript from the library of the Ill.·. Bro.·. F. Astier, 1857.

On last page: "Accurately translated by me from an old French MS. purchased at the sale of the library of the Th.·. Ill.·. Bro.·. Astier, at Paris, in April, 1856. Albert Pike, Rose Croix.·. S.·.P.·.R.·.S.·. Sov.·. Insp.·. Gen.·. 33d. Little Rock, Arkansas, 22d October, 1857."

192 p. Wide 8°. All pages ruled with a border of red. Occasional pen illustrations throughout. Not paged. Bound in full morocco, gilt edges. Lettered "Rituals, 18th, 30th."

NINTH DEGREE OF SCOTTISH MASONRY AND THE FOURTH OF THE CHAPTER OF ROSE CROIX. Elect of the Nine, or Perfect Elect Mason. [Also:]

TENTH DEGREE OF SCOTTISH MASONRY AND THE FIFTH OF THE CHAPTER OF ROSE CROIX. Elect of the Fifteen. [Also:]

ELEVENTH DEGREE OF SCOTTISH MASONRY AND THE SIXTH OF THE CHAPTER OF ROSE CROIX. Sublime Elect or Elect of the Twelve Tribes.

105 written pages. Wide 8°. Before 1879. All pages ruled with a border of red. Not paged. Flexible morocco binding, lettered "IX, X, XI-De Castro."

EIGHTEENTH DEGREE. Ancient and Accepted Scottish Rite. Knight of the Eagle or Pelican, or Sovereign Prince Rose Croix. Revised by C[harles] L[affon] deL[adebat] and A[lbert] P[ike.]. New Orleans, 1858. 188 written p. Wide 8°.

All pages ruled with a border of red. Bound in full morocco and lettered: "Ritual. 18th degree. C. L. deL. & A. P."

THIRTIETH DEGREE. Ancient and Accepted Scottish Rite. The Grand Elect Knight Kadosch.·. or Knight of the White and Black Eagle. Revised by C[harles] L[affon] deL[adebat] and A[lbert] P[ike.] 1858. 139 written p. Wide 8°.

Each page ruled with a border of red. Bound in full morocco and lettered: "Ritual. 30th Degree. C. L. deL. & A. P."

THIRTY-FIRST DEGREE. Ancient and Accepted Scottish Rite. Grand Inspector Inquiring Commander. Revised by C[harles] L[affon] deL[adebat] and A[lbert] P[ike.] 33ds. 1857. 40 written p. 8°. [Also:]

THIRTY-SECOND DEGREE. Ancient and Accepted Scottish Rite. Sublime Prince of the Royal Secret.·. Revised by C[harles] L[affon] deL[adebat] and A[lbert] P[ike.] 33ds. 1857. 137 written p. Wide 8°.

All pages of each MS. ruled with a border of red. Not paged. Bound in full brown morocco, gilt edges, and lettered: "Rituals. 31st & 32.·. C. L. deL. & A. P."

THIRTY-THIRD DEGREE. 153 written pages. Roy. 8°.

No lettering on cover, but pasted thereon is a slip in Pike's hand: "33. Ritual of 1868. Disused in 1880." All pages ruled with a border of red.

SUBSCRIPTION LIST OF OFFICIAL BULLETINS. From vol. 1 to vol. 7. 29 written pages.

Written in a Cash Book of 281 p. Pasted on front cover is the above legend in Pike's own hand.

BIBLIOGRAPHY

THE SYMBOLISM OF THE BLUE DEGREES OF FREEMASONRY. Copied for the author [Albert Pike] by Edwin B. MacGrotty, 33°. Washington, 1888. 400 p. Roy. 8°.

Bound in full blue morocco and lettered on back: "Esoterika. The symbolism of the blue degrees of freemasonry. Property of the Sup[reme] Co[uncil.] Washington, 1888." Of the 400 numbered pages, there are 133 blank pages.

The title page is a work of art, done in blue, black and gold, with a background of a large square and compass. Every word of the text is in imitation of print, none of the letters being joined, while every page is numbered in imitation of printed figures. All pages are of the finest quality of paper and ruled with a border of red.

One other copy of this work is located in the archives of Quatuor Coronati Lodge No. 2076 [Lodge of Research] London, and is described as follows:

"Volume bound in dark blue cloth, with leather back and corners, consisting of 198 sheets of ruled Foolscap paper, of which 195 sheets are hand-written on one side only, and 3 sheets blank. Lettered on the back PIKE'S SYMBOLISM. On sheet 195 is inscribed:

> The foregoing copy is a true copy of a manuscript in the handwriting of General Albert Pike of Washington in the United States of America and was made by the undersigned Brother Reginald Thomas Webster, Solicitor of the Kilburn Lodge 1608 at the dictation of the undersigned George William Speth P.M. Unity 183 and Sec. Quatuor Coronati 2076 and subsequently examined by them with the original.

[Signed] R. E. T. Webster
G. Wm. Speth
9th March 1889
Margate"

See: Records and Minutes of the *Provincial Grand Lodge . . . Royal Order of Scotland,* Washington, 1890, Allocution of the Provincial Grand Master [Albert Pike], p. 370: ". . . after two years had passed I did do the promised work. I have given to the manuscript-book containing it the title 'The Symbolism of the Blue Degrees of Free-Masonry'. . . One copy of the work is here [House of the Temple]; and one, made there from the original manuscript, is in England in the keeping of Bro.·. Gould, the Masonic historian. *No other copy of it or of any part of it can be made,* and the original rough manuscript has been destroyed . . . It will remain always in safekeeping in the House of the Temple . . . because the Royal Order has no home; and it will never be permitted to be taken out of that building . . . If lent to one and another, it would soon be ruined or disappear: for there is no trust to be put in borrowers of books, as I have found to my cost."

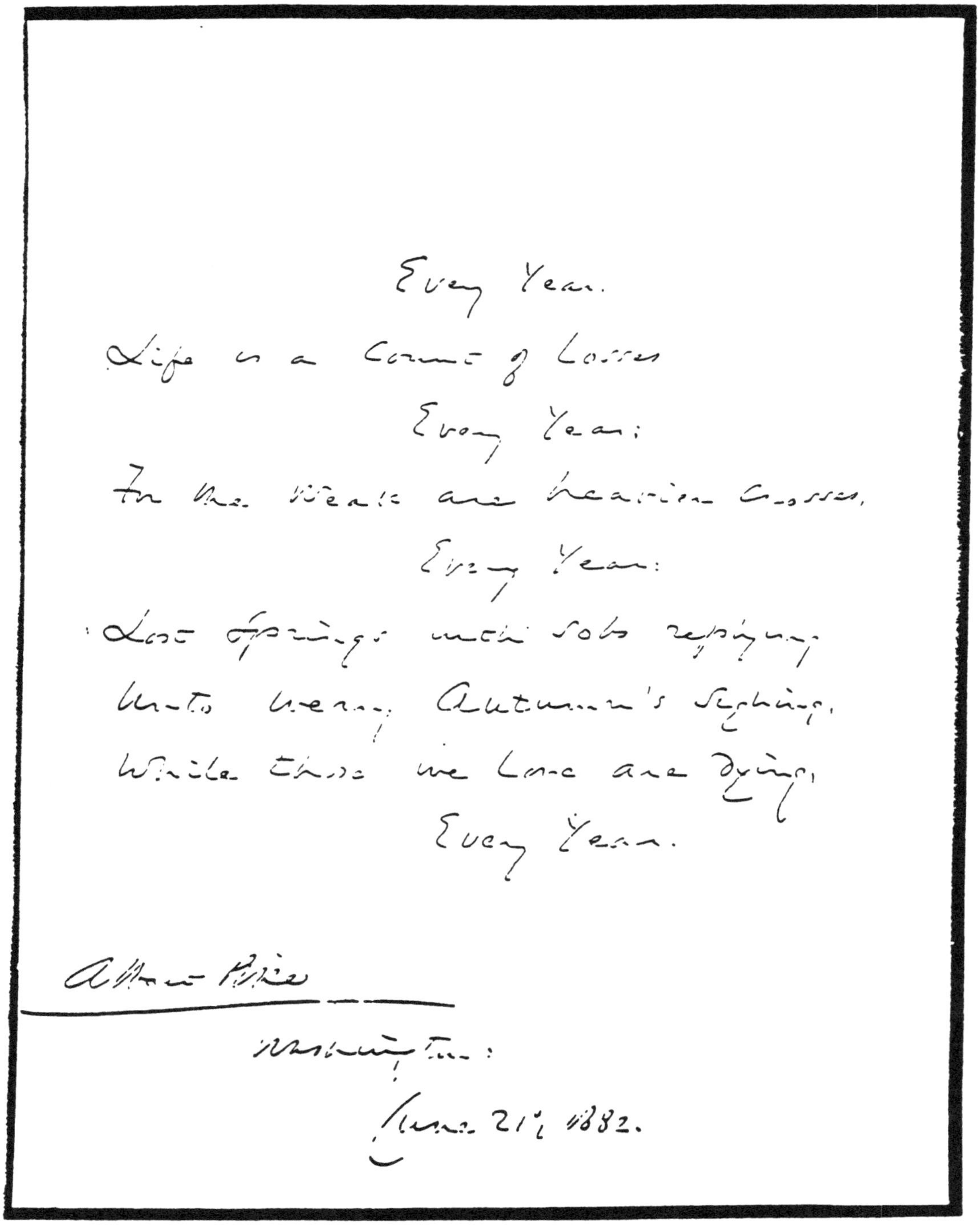

Every Year.

Life is a Count of Losses

Every Year:

For the Weak are heavier Crosses,

Every Year:

Lost Springs with sobs replying

Unto weary Autumn's sighing,

While those we love are dying,

Every Year.

Albert Pike

Washington:

June 21st, 1882.

ON JUNE 21, 1882, ALBERT PIKE WROTE OUT IN LONGHAND A REVISION OF *Every Year* WITH EACH VERSE ON A SEPARATE, BORDERED SHEET, EACH PAGE SIGNED AND DATED. ONE OF THESE IS REPRODUCED ABOVE.

EVERY YEAR

(Albert Pike's Best Known Poem)

Life is a count of losses,
Every year;
For the weak are heavier crosses
Every year:
Lost springs with sobs replying,
Unto weary autumn's sighing,
While those we love are dying,
Every year.

The days have less of gladness,
Every year;
The nights more weight of sadness,
Every year.
Fair springs no longer charm us,
The winds and weather harm us,
The threats of death alarm us,
Every year.

There come new cares and sorrows,
Every year;
Dark days and darker morrows,
Every year;
The ghosts of dead loves haunt us,
The ghosts of changed friends taunt us,
And disappointments daunt us,
Every year.

To the past go more dead faces,
Every year;
As the loved leave vacant places,
Every year;
Every where the sad eyes meet us,
In the evening's dusk they greet us,
And to come to them entreat us,
Every year.

"You are growing old," they tell us,
Every year;
"You are more alone," they tell us,
Every year;
"You can win no more affection;
"You have only recollection,
"Deeper sorrow and dejection,
Every year."

The shores of life are shifting,
Every year;
And we are seaward drifting,
Every year;
Old places, changing, fret us,
The living more forget us,
There are fewer to regret us,
Every year.

But the truer life draws nigher,
Every year;
Its morning star climbs higher,
Every year;
Earth's hold on us grows slighter,
And the heavy burden lighter,
And the dawn immortal brighter,
Every year.

As revised June 21, 1882.

CPSIA information can be obtained
at www.ICGtesting.com
Printed in the USA
LVHW061123300119
605776LV00003B/264/P

9 781564 594488